The Deacon in the Church

THE DEACON IN THE CHURCH

Lynn C. Sherman

ALBA · HOUSE NEW · YORK

SOCIETY OF ST. PAUL, 2187 VICTORY BLVD., STATEN ISLAND, NY 10314

Library of Congress Cataloging-in-Publication Data

Sherman, Lynn C.
The deacon in the church.
p. cm.
ISBN 0-8189-060.7-3
1. Deacons — Catholic Church. 2. Catholic Church — Clergy.
BX1912.D32 1991 90-27863
262'.142 — dc20 CIP

Designed, printed and bound in the United States of America by the Fathers and Brothers of the Society of St. Paul, 2187 Victory Boulevard, Staten Island, New York 10314, as part of their communications apostolate.

PRINTING INFORMATION:

Current Printing - first digit 1 2 3 4 5 6 7 8 9 10 11 12

Year of Current Printing - first year shown
1991 1992 1993 1994 1995 1996 1997 1998

Dedicated to
Jesus Christ the ultimate Deacon,
who gave me my wife Barbara,
my son Roger, my daughter Theresa,
and their love and support
to do His will.

Preface

THE QUESTION is, are you called to service? The answer is yes! Without a doubt, if you are a Christian you are called by Jesus to love and serve your brothers and sisters. If you are a Catholic Christian the same thing is true, plus you are being invited, as in no other time in the Church's history, to be involved with other members of the Mystical Body of Christ in service. If you are a male Catholic Christian (at least at the time of this writing) you may be called to service in a most distinctive way. It is to this unique calling that this book is addressed. The question now becomes, are you called to service in the Catholic Church as an ordained permanent deacon?

The office of permanent deacon, as re-established by the Second Vatican Council, is fairly young, as programs in the Catholic Church are concerned. The initially proposed value of the diaconate in underdeveloped countries has been partially overshadowed by its tremendous growth in the developed industrialized nations. This office is still defining its identity and true role in the modern Church. Accordingly, the permanent diaconate is not fully understood or appreciated in many communities.

This book does not attempt to define permanent diaconate. To some extent, that must be done in each local church community, for that community. What is attempted is a review of what can be documented about the permanent diaconate, who are to be selected for formation, what this formation or training period involves, and the function of deacons. Much of this information will be related to the prime focus of this book, that is, discernment of the vocation, and answering the call to the diaconate.

The man hearing this call, or at least offered the opportunity to think about it, faces the beginning of an exciting journey. Before he embarks he will undoubtedly feel a need for as much information as he can get. There are a number of sources to which he can turn. Several of these may give what he needs, while others will only require more information to explain them. In the following pages a distillation of these resources is offered, along with observations of, and reactions to the permanent diaconate by many who have taken the same journey.

Since discernment doesn't end with acceptance into a diocesan formation program for deacons, training programs will be discussed. The United States National Conference of Bishops has mandated a three year period of training. There are a number of reasons for this length of formation. One of the most important is the need for growth. Growth in turn calls for change and change causes further growth and maturity, or stress and upheaval. There are unique dynamics at play during this time. When understood and used with sincere prayer the result is a more well-rounded and Christ-centered servant to the whole Church.

It is estimated that more than 90% of deacons and candidates in formation are married. (A 1989 national survey of American permanent deacons indicated that 91% were married, 4% celibate, 3% widowed, and 2% divorced.) It is often pointed out that under normal circumstances only permanent deacons will receive all seven sacraments during their lifetime. This only underscores the importance of the sacrament of marriage in the life and ministry of deacons. The approval, support, and involvement by wife and family, on a consistent and continual basis, is required. These pages will hopefully provide answers and information to the entire family of a possible candidate. Just as comments from ordained deacon husbands/fathers are offered to men interested in this vocation, comments from their wives and family members are offered.

As these pages were written, all of the above interests were kept in mind. Additionally, the interests and concerns of priests, religious, and laity who want to know more about this ministry were considered and included. The result is a work not of limited appeal or relevance, but rather something for all members of the modern Church.

Admittedly, this book may slip into a subjective response to this ministry. It is the result of the author's own discernment, formation and new ministry. Where this occurs, Christian forgiveness is begged. In part this is unavoidable, just as everyone's journey in faith is subjective and can only be understood in the context of their life. So, as many personal experiences, observations, and reflections as possible were solicited from others. Bracketed text will be used throughout this book to indicate these reflections. It is earnestly prayed that the end result is of instructional and of spiritual value to those interested in, or called to service as permanent deacons in the Catholic Church.

Deacon Lynn C. Sherman
December 26, 1990
Feast of St. Stephen

Acknowledgments

A WORK of this type cannot be accomplished alone. The author is indebted to a number of people who aided directly or indirectly to this project and whom he wishes to publicly acknowledge and thank.

The true collaborator for this whole project is my loving and patient wife, Barbara. Just as she supported and aided me in my formation and diaconate ministry, she gave me tremendous help with every section of this book, especially the reflective notes. This book would never have been completed if it were not for her. Likewise, my son, Roger, and my daughter, Theresa, helped me by acting as outside critics, insuring that what was written would be understandable to a wide range of readers.

Special prayer and thanks are offered for Archbishop Philip M. Hannan for accepting me into formation, and Archbishop Francis B. Schulte for ordaining me, Reverend Richard N. Maughan, Pastor of Visitation of Our Lady Church, who called me by name and recommended me to the diaconate program, and gave continuous counsel and direction, both to my ministry and this project.

I want to give acknowledgment to and appreciation for the fine staff of the Archdiocese of New Orleans Office of Permanent Diaconate; the Director, Deacon Jim Swiler, assistant Directors Deacon Bill O'Regan and Deacon Tom Caffery, and their most capable secretary, Mrs. Donna Giroir.

There is no way I could fully explain how much each member

of the 1989 New Orleans diaconate class, and their wives have aided in this project. What I received from them I have tried to share with the reader, the realization that you cannot fully respond to this call alone. They are: Douglas and Una Authement, Robert and Fay Binney, Donald and Dottie Bourgeois, SJ and Thais Calamia, Piero and Lido Caserta, Carl and Joey Cleveland, Jere and Kathleen Crago, Charles and Cynthia Duke, Chuck and "Boots" Hartman, Jerry and Kathleen Harrison, Charles and Ann Heine, William and Janice Johnson, Roberto and Molly Jiminez, Raymond and Shirley Lewis, Michael and Lynn Nestor, Harry and Carol Schexnayder, and Daniel and Leatha Vincent.

Each faculty member of the Archdiocese of New Orleans diaconate program deserves the thanks of all whom they have taught, and all whom these deacons will minister to. They are: Deacon Allen Johnson, Rev. Earl F. Neilhus, SM, Deacon Frans Labranche, Jr., Rev. Kenneth Hedrick, Msgr. Ignatius Roppolo, Rev. Reginald R. Masterson, OP, Rev. Frank Montalbano, OMI, Sister Fara Impastato, OP, Sister Patricia Cormack, SCCS, Deacon Thomas E. Caffery, Jr., Deacon Gerald J. Martinez, Deacon Gilbert R. Schmidt, Rev. Joseph P. Mullin, SM, (special thanks for review of the chapter on Canon Law), and Mrs Dianne Ribando.

For the descriptions of their diaconate formation program, I wish to thank: Rev. Frank J. Silva, Director, Archdiocese of Boston, Rev. John O'Donoghue, Director, Archdiocese of San Antonio, Rev. Mr. Thomas Knestout, Archdiocese of Washington, and Rev. Mr. Constantino "Connie" J. Feriola, Jr., Secretary, National Conference of Catholic Bishops Permanent Diaconate Committee.

Sincere appreciation to my Pastoral Director during formation, Deacon Wilfred Robichaux, Jr., and my diaconate "big brother" Deacon Ferris Duet who kept me on track for three and a half years, and my CPT instructor and Spiritual Director, Rev. Hilton Rivet, SJ.

Finally, eternal appreciation and prayers for my primary Spiritual Director, Rev. Pius Lartigue, OSB. May he rest in the presence of the Father, the peace of the Son, and the perpetual grace of the Holy Spirit.

Contents

The Deacon in the Church

I.

What Is The Permanent Diaconate?

IT IS SAFE to say that a week does not go by that each permanent deacon, while ministering to others, is not asked this question. It is also safe to say that there are many active Catholics, and even some priests and religious, who would like a clear answer to this question. There are also a few deacons who would appreciate a good well-worded answer, so that they could use it, as needed, and spend more time ministering rather than explaining their ministry.

This is understandable to all who have experienced the revitalization of the Church as the result of the Second Vatican Council. Many things in the Church that had quick answers have been re-analyzed. The limited question/answer approach to theology and spirituality has given way to more relevant understandings of our faith. Each individual is being called upon to become personally involved in their own faith and salvation. All are being called upon to assist each other. Answers are now coming from the Body of Christ, the faithful in and with the Church, and not just from books.

But how do we answer this question? Not just "very carefully." We answer it from the various perspectives from which this ministry is viewed. To a deacon, ministry is one thing; to the laity, another. In the structure of the Church it is an office, in the home of the needy it is a blessing. The permanent diaconate, like the Church, is many things, but most of all it is *service.*

For those who need a non-academic but very thorough explanation of the diaconate, the following three paragraphs are offered. They are from the letter sent by the Archdiocese of New Orleans' Office of Permanent Diaconate to those persons listed as references, by applicants to the program:

> In case you are not fully acquainted with the Diaconate, it is a permanent order in the Church in the United States which was restored and reestablished by the Bishops in 1968. In our own Archdiocese Deacons are serving in a variety of ministries. Most of these men are married and have children. They practice, in a sense, a tri-vocational status of family life, business, and religious service.
>
> After completing three and one half years of special studies, candidates are ordained by the Archbishop to their permanent order and are then called upon to function on a parish level or within the framework of the Archdiocese. As an indication of the extent of this most serious calling, the Deacon is privileged to preach, to officiate at Baptism and Marriages, he may preside over wake services and Christian burials. He assists the celebrant with the liturgy, distributes the Eucharist, counsels the sick and ministers to the dying.
>
> He is, indeed, a minister of Jesus Christ, of the Church of God.

[Making the decision to apply to the diaconate program took on a new reality the day I submitted the names of three references. I, like most, contacted each of them beforehand. But since this was all new to me, the more I tried to explain it the more confused I became. My boss asked, based on my poor explanation, if I would be quitting to be a priest. Finally understanding that this was not my goal, he then asked what the salary was for being a deacon.]

Father Patrick McCaslin and Mr. Michael G. Lawler recently published a book on the diaconate. The title of their work gives a very insightful definition to "deacon," *A Vision of the Permanent Diaconate Today: Sacrament of Service* (Paulist Press, 1986). In their introduction they write:

> It has long been our concern that any search for the meaning of the diaconate should concentrate on three areas: 1) the humanity of Jesus; 2) the nature of the Church; 3) the Catholic notion of sacramentality. We have attempted to pursue that concentration in this book, hoping to show that any practical conclusions about the diaconate should be derived from sound theological bases, and not just from the functional pragmatism we hear all around us today. By functional pragmatism we mean a statement such as: 'Any lay person can do anything a deacon can do, so why ordain deacons?' As a statement about a functionary, that statement can get by; but as a statement about a sacrament, which we believe and shall argue that a deacon is, it makes as much theological sense as the statement that pouring water on people makes them nothing but wet. It is an ancient teaching in the Catholic tradition that sacrament presupposes faith, and is useless without it. In this book we shall consistently present deacons as sacraments and not just as functionaries, and insist that faith is necessary to see beyond the functionary to the sacrament and what it symbolizes.

The understanding of sacrament then becomes important to the understanding of the diaconate. Father McCaslin and Mr. Lawler go into great detail to explain Jesus as the Sacrament of God. The Church is then seen as a sacrament of Jesus, and each one of us, as members of the Chruch and the Mystical Body of Christ, are part of that living sacrament. "To serve, not to be served," is realized as the identifying characteristic and calling of Christ's life, and the life of the Church. The Greek word *diakonia*, service, labels this characteristic, and that particular Holy Order.

While this approach to an understanding of diaconate is valid, it may not be an easy starting point for everyone. The functional concept they rejected may be easier to handle. For example, we often define something by its powers. The President of the United States, or the role of Congressman can be defined and explained by the powers each has. Machines, computers, systems, programs, and even professions are often described by what they can do, their powers. Even the priesthood is defined in the popular media by its powers.

It is not surprising, then, to find many trying to explain the restored permanent diaconate in this way. To say that a deacon can perform all the sacraments but the Eucharist, Reconciliation, and Anointing of the Sick, and he can wear an alb and stole while performing liturgical functions is as easy as it is incomplete. Defining this ministry only by its powers not only does it an injustice, but it is very misleading. The prime focus of *diakonia*, service, is completely overlooked. The "powers" become an end rather than a means to an end.

The discussion of the permanent deacon's authorization and empowerment is appropriate for discussion, but it cannot be accepted as the most important factor in reaching an understanding of this office. The functions of a deacon, not his faculties, are the important points. More directly, how he ministers to others, for the Church, for Jesus Christ gives the answer to the question, "What is the permanent diaconate?"

II.

The Diaconate In History

THE OFFICE OF DEACON is almost as old as the Church itself. The Acts of the Apostles, Chapter 6 spells out clearly the perceived need for them, their selection, and installation into a position of service. As one modern observer commented in making the point that the diaconate is rooted in service, ''If you had to write a want ad for the first deacons it would have to read: Wanted - seven wise and prayerful men to wait on tables, bilingual preferred.'' (See Ac 6:1-6).

The spread of this office is evident from several other New Testament references. While the Twelve Apostles (Ac 6) call on new deacons to only be ''deeply spiritual and prudent,'' St. Paul gives further instructions in the matter:

> In the same way deacons must be serious, straightforward, and truthful. They may not overindulge in drink or give in to greed. They must hold fast to the divinely revealed faith with a clear conscience. They should be put on probation first; then, if there is nothing against them, they may serve as deacons. (1 Tm 3:8-10)
>
> Deacons may be married but once and must be good managers of their children and their households. Those who serve well as deacons gain a worthy place themselves and much assurance in their faith in Christ Jesus. (1 Tm 3:12-13)

These attributes will be discussed later as they relate to the selection and formation process for modern permanent deacons. What is significant in an historical perspective is the clear concept of the diaconate during the earliest days of the Church. During the first several decades, it is hard to distinguish the presbyterate and the episcopate. The bishops, following the example of the Apostles, focused their efforts on "prayer and the ministry of the word" (Ac 6:4). The order of deacons in each local church community made this possible by its ministry of service.

Of course the emergence of the presbyters, priests, did not eliminate the theological or practical reasons for deacons. As St. Ignatius of Antioch wrote: "The bishop images the Father, presbyters image the Apostles, and deacons image Jesus Christ." The shift in perception was, and is logical.

For about the first eight centuries of the Church's history, the deacon worked in an ever widening circle of responsibilities. This history is best thought of as a series of vaguely parallel lines that continue to branch off, and connect with each other, or stray off on their own course. It is a history still needing further research and review. The names and stories of numerous deacons who ultimately joined the ranks of the canonized are fairly well documented. It is from these that much can be learned today. The tales of the lesser individuals of this order, and the outright scandalous, who played their part in the dissolution of it as a permanent office, demonstrate what must be avoided.

The restored permanent diaconate must be viewed in the context of the Church today. That is unquestionable. Nevertheless, two quotes immediately come to mind when discussing its history. The first is the old adage, "He who is ignorant of the lessons of history is condemned to repeat them." The other is a comment by Pope John XXIII describing the most dangerous man in the Church as the one who believes that what has been for the past 50 years must be the way it always was.

Looking at the earliest history of the diaconate, and subsequently, its later years before being discontinued as a permanent order, is helpful in understanding its role in the Church today. The required attributes for deacons still stand, as do the types of ministries they are best suited for. It is also important to relate the early evolution of the diaconate to that of the episcopacy and of the presbyterate.

a) Priest And Deacon Development

The question, "What is a deacon?" is more often asked and answered today than the question, "What is a priest?" Yet, the answering of one question helps answer the other. The history of the presbyters, priests, relates to needs and developments in the early Church. So does the diaconate.

This process of awareness and change is discussed by Richard P. McBrien in his book *Catholicism*:

> Not until the early Christians concluded that they were indeed part of a radically new movement distinct from Judaism was there a basis for the development of a separate Christian priesthood. Other events accentuated this process: the increasing number of Gentile converts, the shift of leadership away from the Jerusalem Church, and to the churches of Rome, Antioch, Ephesus, and Alexandria, the destruction of the Temple, and finally, Judaism's own sectarian tendencies in the post-destruction period. Concomitantly, there was a growing recognition of the sacrificial character of the Eucharist, which called for a priesthood of sacrifice distinct from the Jewish priesthood. This awareness appeared in Christian writings about the end of the first century or the beginning of the second

especially in the Didache, in the writings of Clement of Rome (d. 100), and in the Apostolic Tradition of St. Hippolytus of Rome (d. ca. 236).

The modern priesthood has its roots in the presbyterate of the very early Church, and as time passed the theological implications of this office became clearer.

Much the same can be said of the diaconate. It evolved within the context of its original image, service to the local church community. As the concept of a monarchical episcopacy was accepted, that is, a local church being presided over and identified by one bishop, the diaconate took on related characteristics. St. Hippolytus indicates in his third century writings that bishops were elected by the people, but they received the imposition of hands by another bishop. Priests, he wrote, were ordained by a bishop with other priests present. Deacons, on the other hand, were ordained by the bishop alone, since they were to be in the service of the bishop. While all of the Holy Orders are directed towards the order of the local church, this order, diaconate, was directed by the bishop towards the service of the Church.

The serving at tables, recounted in the Acts of the Apostles, was just the beginning. Feeding the hungry and distributing alms to the needy expanded to the managing of all the charitable efforts of the local church. "That some, if not all, members of the diaconal college were everywhere stewards of the church funds and of the alms collected for widows and orphans is beyond dispute." (*The Catholic Encyclopedia*, 1908 ed. s.v. "Deacon")

b. Deacon Lawrence

This responsibility was admirably carried out by St. Lawrence, a deacon to Pope Sixtus II. In 258 A.D. he responded to the Roman Emperor Valerian's slaying of Sixtus, and an attempt to seize the treasures of the Church by spending it all on the poor. St. Lawrence presented Valerian with a gathering of the blind, widows, orphans, the elderly, lepers, and the lame, saying, "Here are the true treasures of the Church."

The writer Prudentius tells us how this story turned out. A red-hot griddle was prepared by Valerian's men, and Lawrence was tied to it. In the midst of this unbelievable torture Lawrence is reported to have instructed his executioners to turn him over because he was broiled enough on one side. (This is possibly the first recorded example of diaconal humor in the face of adversity.)

c. Deacons In Early Church Writings

Much of the early history of this office can be pieced together from assorted letters, Council canons, and theological writings of the day. While this book does not attempt to give a comprehensive history of the diaconate, a few historical notes are of interest. (Taken from *The Book of Catholic Quotations*, edited by John Chapin, 1956.)

In about the middle of the second century, a work entitled *The Teaching of the Twelve Apostles*, also called the *Didache*, gives an insight into the standards set for deacons as well as bishops:

> Elect therefore, for yourselves, bishops and deacons worthy of the Lord, humble men and not covetous, and faithful and well tested, for they also serve you in the ministry of the prophets and teachers.

St. Ignatius of Antioch, in his *Letter to the Magnesians*, wrote on the hierarchal structure of the Church, and the position and function of deacons:

> I exhort you to be careful to do all things in the harmony of God, the bishop having primacy after the model of God and the priests after the model of the council of Apostles, and the deacons (who are so dear to me) having entrusted to them the ministry of Jesus Christ.

Today's approximately 8,000 deacon's wives will find Canon 3 of the Council of Nicaea, 325 A.D. interesting:

> The great synod has stringently forbidden any bishop, presbyter, deacon, or any one of the clergy whatever, to have a woman dwelling with him, except only his mother, sister, aunt, or such person as are beyond all suspicion.

The Church's Fathers now see things differently than in the fourth century. Today the sacrament of Marriage is understood as a support to diaconal ministry. Canon 9 of the Council of Rome, 386 A.D. reveals how much things have changed:

> We advise that priests and deacons should not live with their wives.

(It is interesting to find out how many couples have never discussed with each other if they would remarry if the other were to die. The present prohibition against remarriage by deacons can bring up this topic, but as a one-sided discussion. Only the wife can remarry. My wife, Barbara, says she would not.)

The beginnings of a celibate clergy find their legal roots during this time period, although as a norm in many local churches it began much earlier. The point here is that as clerics, deacons were held to a different set of standards than the rest of the Church. The fourth century Ecclesiastical Canon of the Holy Apostles contained the following:

> He who has been married twice after his baptism, or has had a concubine, cannot be made a bishop, or presbyter, or deacon, or indeed anyone of the sacerdotal catalogue.

(Those familiar with the exploits and later life of one Augustine of Hippo will realize how this rule could have affected St. Monica's son if it were a universal rule. There is no telling how much Church history and theology would have been different.)

A glimpse of the Eastern Church gives some insight into one of the parallel lines of development of the clergy during the early Church. The Eastern Orthodox Church has retained the permanent diaconate into modern times. For a look at how the roots of this order began we quote Canon 6 of the Quinisext Council of Constantinople, 692 A.D., as recorded in the Norms for the Eastern Church:

> Since it is declared in the apostolic canons that of those who are advanced to the clergy unmarried, only lectors and cantors are able to marry, we also, maintaining this, determine that henceforth it is in no way lawful for any subdeacon, deacon, or presbyter after his ordination to contract matrimony; but if he shall have dared to do so, let him be deposed. And if any of those who enter the clergy wishes to be joined to a wife in lawful marriage before he is ordained subdeacon, deacon, or presbyter, let it be done.

d. Deacons As Clergy

The question of who is clergy and who is not has different answers from different ages, and from different local churches.

Present canon law defines clergy to include bishops, priests, and deacons. The preceding Code of 1917 included as clergy: bishops, priests, deacons, subdeacons, and the four minor orders of porter, lector, exorcist, and acolyte. Lector and acolyte are now lay ministries. Local law and initiative have taken over the regulation of porter, exorcist, and catechist. The subdiaconate has been dropped to the equivalent of the lay ministry of acolyte. A discussion of clergy will be presented in the section of this book dealing with specific canons that relate to the diaconate, directly or indirectly.

As can be seen from these historical references, the Church has always tried to make itself as effective as possible in its mission here on earth. To do this it set down qualifications, definitions, duties, rules, and regulations for its ministers and laity. As civilization became more complex, so did the infrastructure of the Church. Tracing the history of the diaconate is a study in the organizational evolution of the Church itself, although a peripheral one.

Concerns for stability and the chaste lifestyle of its prime officials translated into local and universal Church rules on clerical marriage and celibacy. The very identity of the clergy required appropriate guidelines for the selection of suitable candidates, and their personal attributes. The ever present problems of "being in the world but apart from it" generated literally hundreds of canons in each age, many aimed at governing the clergy.

e. Vesture

As was mentioned earlier, ministerial offices, and even professions are often defined by their powers. They are likewise identified by their uniforms or vestments. Well into the sixth century, the Christian clergy wore no distinctive garb to set them apart from the laity, on a day to day basis. It was about this time that the general public adopted shorter tunics. The clergy retained the old Roman long tunic, a precursor of the cassock.

Liturgical vesture, by and large, was the adaptation of customary dress which over a period of time became more stylized and/or symbolic.

For the deacon the dalmatic became the identifying vestment. A simple over-the-head tunic of square cut and sleeves, it was open on the sides and extended to the knees. It was characterized by two vertical stripes, clavi. Liturgically, in earlier times these stripes were different colors for different ranks of the hierarchy. The dalmatic is said to have received its name from the Dalmatian wool first used to make them. Some scholars identify it as a fashion brought over to Rome from Dalmatia, where it was primarily worn by the "well to do."

Joseph Dahmus writes in the *Dictionary of Medieval Civilization*:

> In early centuries it was worn by bishops, and from the fourth century by deacons as well. From the twelfth century its public use was largely restricted to deacons, although bishops and other dignitaries continue to wear it under the chasuble.

The stole, a strip of cloth worn about the neck, is another clerical identifier. Today both priests and deacons wear a stole over their alb as normal vestments for liturgical services. Priests wear the stole around their neck with both ends hanging down in front of them. Deacons wear it over their left shoulder, and across their body to the right side below the hip. *The New Catholic Encyclopedia* reports that the origin of the stole is obscure, but was already in use in the East by the fourth century as an insignia of the lower clergy. It was adapted, apparently, from the Imperial civil services as a mark of authority. "First record of its use is always in council and synodal decrees as a distinctive mark for deacons, later for priests and bishops."

The manner in which the stole is worn by deacons today is not an adaptation of the priestly norm. There are numerous drawings, illustrations in manuscripts, paintings, and mosaics from the period between the eighth and eleventh centuries that show deacons wearing their stole hung straight down from their left shoulder. The ''Exultet Roll'' at the cathedral at Bari, Italy, is a fine example of this practice.

f. Papal Deacons

Another resource for information on the history of the diaconate is contained in the Roman Martyrology, and the catalog of saints. It is reassuring to find a good number of deacons and elevated deacons on these lists. This number may be larger than expected since many of the early saints were popes. It should be remembered that as the Bishop of Rome, the Pope had his own deacons serve as administrators of that local church. In large dioceses, like Rome, one deacon was put in charge of the work done by the other deacons. This cleric was called the archdeacon. They were both administrators, and confidants to the popes. Their elevation was not only operationally sound, but spiritually supportable.

Some, but not all, of the pope/saints that were permanent deacons prior to elevation are (compiled from *The Dictionary of Saints*):

St. Agapitus (d. 536) was a Roman archdeacon when elected pope.

St. Callistus I (d.c. 222) was ordained a deacon in 199, and was elected Pope in 217 in a disputed election.

St. Celestine I (d. 432) was a friend of St. Augustine; he was a deacon in Rome, elected to the papacy in 422.

St. Damasus I (c. 384) was the son of a priest. He became a Roman deacon, but when elected Pope in 366 faced an anti-pope.

St. Gregory I, the Great (d.c. 604) was a deacon from 578 to 590, when elected Pope. A great reformer, a Latin Doctor of the Church.

St. Leo I, the Great (d. 461) was famous for dissuading Attila the Hun from attacking Rome. A deacon to Pope Celestine I and Sixtus III.

St. Leo IV (d. 855) was deacon to Pope Gregory IV, and made Cardinal by Pope Sergius II, whom he succeeded in 847.

St. Leo IX (d. 1054), while a deacon, served in the military. He was elected Bishop of Toul, and later elected Pope in 1049.

St. Nicholas I (d. 867) was deacon to Pope Leo IV before his papacy.

St. Siricius (d. 399) was a Roman deacon elected Pope in 384.

g. Deacon Saints

The reader may wish to seek out the biographies of these saints. Their lives are not only informative, but inspirational. They were men of their day, facing the problems, and sometimes persecutions of their times. Each responded to the call of Our Lord in a very special way. One thing that comes through the edifying accounts of their lives is their humanity. They were men called to a mission, but they were men first.

Some of the other canonized deacons of note include the widely known and the lesser known. Their stories also help answer the questions, "What is a deacon?" and "What do deacons do?" — both for their times, and ours.

They include, but are not limited to:

St. Stephen, one of the seven first deacons, whose story is recounted in Chapters 6 and 7 of the Acts of the Apostles.

St. Lawrence (d. 258) whose story was told earlier, and who never lived long enough to succeed Pope Sixtus II. (Author's note: The job of Pope, for the first 300 plus years had its drawbacks. No Pope during that time died of natural causes. Each was martyred for the faith. Retirement plans had not been thought of yet.)

St. Apollonius (d.c. 305) was the deacon who converted the musician Philemon, and was sewn in a sack and thrown into the sea for his faith.

St. Athanasius (d. 373), as a deacon, attended the Council of Nicaea; later he was elected Bishop of Alexandria. He is a Doctor of the Church.

St. Bertrand (d.c. 623) was a deacon in Paris, and later Bishop of LeMans.

St. Domitius (d.c. 362) was a Persian convert. He was ordained a deacon and later became a hermit. Still he drew great crowds of people because of his holiness, which ultimately caused him to be stoned to death by Julian the Apostate.

St. Ennondius (d. 521) was married for several years. When he was ordained deacon by St. Epiphanius, his wife became a nun. He was appointed Bishop of Ticinum in 514.

St. Ephraem (d.c. 373) attended the Council of Nicaea as a deacon. He wrote against heretics. He is a Doctor of the Church.

St. Boniface (d. 484) was a deacon in Capsa, Africa. He was ordered to embrace Arianism by King Nuneric, who ultimately put him to death along with St. Liberatus.

St. Raymond of Penafort (d. 1275) was an archdeacon of great learning who later became a Dominican, and confessor to Pope Gregory IX.

St. Thomas Becket (1118-1170) is widely known. He was less than an exemplary Archdeacon of Canterbury. He was made Chancellor of England in 1155 by his good friend King Henry II, who later nominated him to be Archbishop in 1161. Thomas objected, but he was ordained a priest the day before being consecrated bishop. He then led a holy life and became a martyr.

St. Tiburius (d.c. 288) was a victim of the Diocletian persecutions. He reportedly was made to walk on burning coals, but when that did not harm him he was beheaded for the faith.

These are only some of the more notable deacons in Church history. They are offered here as another point of perspective. Again, this is not only edifying to a man discerning if he has a vocation to this order, but it is also of interest to anyone trying to come to terms with the permanent diaconate because of their own needs.

Just as one can learn from the lives of the saints who became deacons, much can be learned from those who were not deacons. The story of St. Matthias being selected to replace Judas as one of the Twelve immediately comes to mind. The first Chapter of the Acts of the Apostles reports that Matthias met all the requirements for the position; he was one of their company from the baptism of Jesus by John through the Ascension. We can therefore assume that he was one of the disciples, and an outstanding one at that.

Matthias' story is of value not so much because he was selected as a replacement Apostle, but rather because he was not selected earlier. Just as many are called, many apply to candidacy for the permanent diaconate. In both cases, not all are chosen. The faithfulness of Matthias was rewarded, as will that of all who place their trust in the Will of God.

[There were 84 couples in attendance at the first Discernment meeting that my wife and I attended. There were approximately 40 who submitted applications. Only 20 were selected. Two years later several of those who had previously applied submitted their applications again, and two of those were selected for formation.]

III.

The Rise And Fall Of The Diaconate

MUCH HAS BEEN WRITTEN about the restoration of the permanent diaconate in the modern Catholic Church. Encyclicals, episcopal guidelines, monographs, and numerous magazine articles all recount the how and why of restoration. The one thing lacking in the majority of these has been a comprehensive answer as to why this restoration was needed in the first place. Why wasn't this "permanent" order permanent enough to make it through the Middle Ages? Exactly what caused its discontinuance as a permanent part of the Church's hierarchy?

The importance of these questions is found in the wisdom of that old adage: "He who is ignorant of the lessons of history is condemned to repeat them."

What then is the answer? Where do we look? Can we pinpoint when the "fall" took place?

Admittedly, many modern writers refer to the abuses of power and position by deacons in the Middle Ages as a cause for the situation requiring restoration. But this fails to give an adequate explanation. The review of the historical circumstances in which the diaconate existed during different periods reveals a more complete answer. Political, social, and theological factors, when taken separately, point to a chain of events that inevitably turned the diaconate into a transitional step toward the priesthood.

In the early 1950's, Wilhelm Schamoni wrote a treatise (*Familienvater als geweith Diakone*), that was translated into English by Dr. Otto Eisner in 1955 under the title *Married Men as Ordained Deacons.* Not only does this pre-Vatican II monograph propose the restoration of the diaconate as a permanent order, but it gives a very insightful analysis of why it became transitional. Even in his preface Schamoni addresses this issue with a poignant reference to the works of charity, *caritas*, as a primary task of the Church, and how its de-emphasis affected the diaconate. He wrote:

> When explaining the development by which the diaconate became a mere transition phase on the way to the priesthood, one point, I think, wants to be more closely examined. It is the transformation of social and economic conditions, caused by Germanic conquerors and landlords, and its importance for the functions of Church *caritas* and, thus, of deacons. It would seem that the transition, at the beginning of the Middle Ages, from an urban money economy of free, equal slave-owning citizens to an agrarian, natural, domestic consumer economy, and the establishment of the Germanic feudal system, did away with the town proletariat without having, to the same extent, brought into being a rural proletariat, because the serfs depended for marriage on the permission of their landlords. The close adherence to the soil did not, it would seem, admit of a proletarianization of the land when conditions became more stable and when the relationship of the Germanic landlord to the Romanized population of the West became more patriarchally Christian. The tasks of the Church were, at that time, less concerned with *caritas*, and that, perhaps, is the main reason why the diaconate, as a lifelong calling, ceased to exist; the Church had, above all, to protect the weak against abuse by the powerful in those days when state authority was unable to protect life and property.

It must be remembered that nothing in the Church happens quickly. Many events during the first thousand years of the Church are more easily measured in decades and centuries, rather than in years. The discontinuance of the diaconate as a permanent order did not happen overnight, nor was it simultaneously church-wide. Like its establishment during the post-apostolic period, it took time.

a. The Rise

The rise of the diaconate was one of the many elements that helped develop a community of disciples into the new Christian Church. Each event recounted in the Acts of the Apostles marked a new need. Some of these needs were spiritual, some were theological, and some were simply operational. The need to have someone wait on tables, so that the Apostles could tend to the spiritual needs of the faithful, was answered by the establishment of the diaconate (Ac 6:1-6). The need to get the good news to more and more people was answered by the preaching of these new ministers of service (Ac 6:7).

Over the next three hundred years the Church grew, was cut back by persecutions, and then grew again. The order of the episcopacy, that of bishop, was established to be the "apostle to each local church community." The order of the presbyterate, that of priest, found its role in aiding the bishop during the liturgy and in serving as his liturgical representative.

Deacons were, during these times, the functional arm of the local bishop, who based his ministry in an urban setting. As time passed, and the Church spread outward from the cities, two types of deacon developed. The first we will call "episcopal deacons" and the other "rural deacons."

Deacons who were attached to a bishop took on many of the administrative tasks of the local church. They received monies and goods. They sought out those in need and distributed aid. They represented the bishop on many occasions and assisted him during the liturgy. Each of these tasks became more involved and more formalized with each passing age. In time deacons exercised both ecclesial and temporal powers. They controlled the growing wealth of the Church. They became the bishop's advisor, legal representative, and confidant. (In the list of deacons who became saints, there are several who attended and participated in Church Councils.) They were often the most logical choice to succeed the bishop upon his natural death or martyrdom.

As the role of the priest increased within the Church, so did the potential rivalry with the order of deacons. To some it became more and more intolerable to have deacons, who were of a lower order than priests, exercise the bishop's power even if it were done so legitimately. The abuses of power and position mentioned in available literature were all that was needed to justify change in local churches. By the Middle Ages there were enough of these localized situations to make it a church-wide issue. It became a political problem that resulted in a political solution.

Here attention is turned to the rural deacons, circa 400-550 A.D. They are similar in many characteristics to the permanent deacons of today. These clerics worked in the local congregations, often with priests. They were removed from the bishop's immediate activity either by distance or ministry. They ministered to the sick, widowed, and orphaned on the parish level. Like their episcopal counterparts, they assisted in the liturgy, but beside a priest rather than a bishop.

b. The Problems

This then was the pattern of development for the diaconate. It saw the rise and fall of the Roman Empire, the Dark Ages, feudalism, the birth of nations, and numerous crusades. Its own rise set the stage for its fall. The economic reasons for the fall are found in both the cities and the rural areas. The political reasons are found primarily with the episcopal deacons.

To be independent, the clergy needed to be self-sufficient. Bishops and priests were maintained by the local church. Deacons, at least in the beginning, had secular trades or occupations to sustain them. Episcopal deacons were the first to be granted Church support in exchange for their ever-increasing responsibilities. As a formalized organization, the Church became the dispenser of spiritual and administrative services. Stipends or contributions in exchange for these services became the norm. Just as deacons became rivals of the priests for the power associated with the managing of increasing Church revenues, they became rivals for stipends.

By 1000 A.D. social changes also led to the fall of the permanent diaconate. The development of monastic communities, hospitals, orphanages, and state support to the needy eliminated many of the deacon's ministries. Those tasks that justified this order as a ministry of *caritas* were taken over by others. This meant the deacon's role was being slowly limited to the liturgy.

Theology, or rather its evolving understanding, then became another reason for the "fall." Just as it took decades of theological pondering to reveal the Eucharist as an unbloody sacrifice requiring a presider (a priest) to officiate over it, the understanding of the liturgy of the Mass took centuries. First there was the monthly Mass for the entire local church, celebrated by the bishop. This evolved into the weekly Mass, by either the bishop or the local priest. The spiritual efficacy of this highest form of prayer prompted not only optional daily Mass, but ultimately in more recent centuries mandated daily Mass to be celebrated by priests. The theological shift from the Eucharistic celebration for the entire community, to a Mass for a specific reason is evident in the rubrics used in different ages. The people of post-apostolic times understood the prayers being offered by and for them when the celebration was in their common language. Their descendants had to be represented symbolically by acolytes, or altar boys, by the time the Mass was standardized in Latin. This process of development ultimately allowed for the "private Mass." As a result, the deacon was no longer necessary in the day to day liturgical life of the local church or parish.

c. The Fall

Put this all together and there is only one logical solution; get rid of the problem group that no longer had any viable reason for existing. The question, though, was: How can one abolish what was established by the Apostles? The answer was simple. Keep it, but make it transitional toward membership in the stronger political constituency. Have deacons become priests.

This did not happen all at once, everywhere. There isn't a specific date to commemorate the "fall." Each bishop facing the situations described above reacted in his own way, for only his diocese. For example, if a particular bishop had a deacon who was too popular, or overly political or disobedient, could he not ordain him a priest and ship him off to a backwoods village parish? These actions slowly developed into a pattern that resulted in a more universal way of doing things. Not being resisted, these actions were supported by a populace that came to prefer being ministered to by priests, rather than by lowly deacons.

Wilhelm Schamoni concluded his well-researched analysis of the history of the diaconate in the rural areas by saying:

> So, in the transitional period between antiquity and the early Middle Ages, when the Church expanded into the country areas, the deacon did great work as precursor and pioneer of the priest in the filial churches; by virtue of his ordination, he acted as leader of the community. As a general rule, however this stage of development continued only in unimportant centers where conditions were unfavorable. Since he had no authority over the keys [i.e., he could not absolve sins] and could not consecrate the Eucharist (although he could distribute it), the deacon was, sooner or later, replaced by the priest.

What lessons are to be learned for the permanent diaconate in the post-Vatican II Church? For one thing, their role is not, and cannot be allowed to be perceived as in competition with the rest of the hierarchy. As the name implies, deacons are servers to all the Church, clerics and laity alike. Secondly, the call to *caritas* must be responded to in ever more unique and effective ways. Institutes of care (hospitals, nursing homes, shelters of the homeless, etc.) are no longer operated solely by religious communities. These state facilities need a deacon's presence, just as individual homes in the parish do. Finally, Vatican II has brought us back to the original understanding of the Eucharist as a community celebration. Permanent deacons should be part of any liturgical celebration that brings Jesus to the people, and the people to God. But this role in the community must be a backdrop to the deacon's primary charism, service.

IV.

The Restoration Of The Permanent Diaconate

THE RESTORATION of the permanent diaconate was approved by the Second Vatican Council, as is recorded in the Dogmatic Constitution on the Church, *Lumen Gentium*, on November 21, 1964. Drawing on the rich traditions of the Church, the "Constitutions of the Egyptian Church," and the writings of St. Polycarp and St. Ignatius of Antioch, the conciliar fathers wrote:

> At a lower level of the hierarchy are to be found deacons, who receive the imposition of hands 'not unto the priesthood, but unto the ministry.' For, strengthened by sacramental grace they are dedicated to the People of God, in conjunction with the bishop and his body of priests, in the service of the liturgy, of the Gospel and of works of charity. It pertains to the office of a deacon, in so far as it may be assigned to him by the competent authority, to administer Baptism, in the name of the Church, to be custodian and distributor of the Eucharist, in the name of the Church, to assist at and bless marriages, to bring Viaticum to the dying, to read the sacred scriptures to the faithful, to instruct and exhort the people, to preside over the worship and the prayer of the faithful, to administer sacramentals, and to officiate at funerals and burial services. Dedicated to works of charity and

> functions of administration, deacons should recall the admonitions of St. Polycarp: 'Let them be merciful, and zealous, and let them walk according to the truth of the Lord, who became the servant of all.'
>
> Since, however, the laws and customs of the Latin Church in force today in many areas render it difficult to fulfill these functions, which are so extremely necessary for the life of the Church, it will be possible in the future to restore the diaconate as a proper and permanent rank of the hierarchy. But it pertains to the competent local episcopal conferences, of one kind or another, with the approval of the Supreme Pontiff, to decide whether and where it is opportune that such deacons be appointed. Should the Roman Pontiff think, it will be possible to confer this diaconal order even upon married men, provided they be of more mature age, and also on suitable young men, for whom however, the law of celibacy must remain in force. (L.G. 29)

With this statement the foundation was laid for the restored diaconate. Like the restoration of a venerable old building, it would take a lot of study, planning, and hard work to bring it back to full and lasting usefulness. To say something is restored is much easier than restoring it. The three major steps taken in Rome to accomplish this goal are recounted in the United States National Conference of Catholic Bishops, *Permanent Deacons in the United States: Guidelines on Their Formation and Ministry*, a must reading for all interested in the diaconate. In 1967, Pope Paul VI issued his letter *Sacrum Diaconatus Ordinem* setting the canonical norms for this office. In June of 1968 the new rites of ordination were promulgated in *Pontificalis Romani Recognito*. Then on August 15, 1972, Pope Paul VI issued his letter *Ad Pacendum* containing norms for the order of permanent diaconate.

In this apostolic letter, His Holiness speaks of the position of the diaconate in the early Church, and what led to its discontinuance as a permanent order. He then wrote:

> As a consequence, the permanent diaconate almost entirely disappeared in the Latin Church. It is scarcely the place to mention the decrees of the Council of Trent proposing to restore the sacred orders in accordance with their own nature as ancient functions within the Church; it was much later that the idea matured of restoring this important sacred order also as a truly permanent rank. Our predecessor Pius XII briefly alluded to this matter. Finally, the Second Vatican Council supported the wishes and requests that, where such would lead to the good of souls, the permanent diaconate should be restored as an intermediate order between the higher ranks of the Church's hierarchy and the rest of the people of God, as an expression of the needs and desires of the Christian communities, as a driving force for the Church's service of Diaconia towards the local Christian communities, and as a sign or sacrament of the Lord Christ himself, who came 'not to be served but to serve.'

While these events were taking place the bishops of the United States studied the matter, and filed a petition to the Holy See asking to be allowed to restore the permanent diaconate in this country. Approval was received on August 30, 1968. In furtherance of the proposal the Bishop's Committee on the Permanent Diaconate was established later that year. This committee drew up the *Guidelines* for selection of candidates, and their formation in preparation for ordination. The first such ordinations were in May and June of 1971.

As can readily be seen, the diaconate in this country is truly young. The above notations, though, give an incomplete impression of what prompted and what took place during this restoration.

At this point a clear understanding of what "restoration" means within the Church is in order. One of the best expressions of this concept comes from John Cardinal Ratzinger, Prefect of the Sacred Congregation of the Doctrine of the Faith. The book *The Ratzinger Report* (Ignatius Press, San Francisco, 1985) copies part of one of the Cardinal's letters on the subject:

Above all I should simply like to recall what I really said: there is no return to the past. A restoration understood thus is not only impossible but also not even desirable. The Church moves forward to the consummation of history, she looks ahead to the Lord who is coming. If, however, the term 'restoration' is understood according to its semantic content, that is to say as a recovery of lost values, within a new totality, then I would like to say that this is precisely the task that imposes itself today in the second phase of the post-conciliar period. Yet, the word 'restoration' is linguistically laden in such a way for us moderns that it is difficult to atttribute this meaning to it. In reality it literally means the same as the word 'reform,' a term that has a wholly different sound to us today. Perhaps I can clarify the matter with an example taken from history. For me Charles Borromeo is the classic expression of a real reform, that is to say, of a renewal that leads forward precisely because it teaches how to live the permanent values in a new way, bearing in mind the totality of the Christian fact and the totality of man.

It can certainly be said that Charles Borromeo rebuilt ('restored') the Catholic Church, which also in the area around Milan was at that time nearly destroyed for awhile, without making a return to the Middle Ages. On the contrary, he created a modern form of the Church. How little 'restorative' such a reform was is seen, for example, in the fact that Charles suppressed a religious order that was nearly in decline and assigned its goods to new, live communities. Who today possesses a similar courage to declare that which is interiorly dead (and continues to live only exteriorly) belongs definitely to the past and must be entrusted with clarity to the energies of the new era? Often new phenomena of Christian awakening are resisted precisely by the so-called reformers, who in their turn spasmodically defend institutions that continue to exist only in contradiction with themselves.

In Charles Borromeo, therefore, we can also see what I meant to say with 'reform' or 'restoration' in its original meaning: to live outstretched toward a totality, to live from a 'yes' that

> leads back to the unity of the human forces in conflict with each other. A 'yes' that confers on them a positive meaning within the totality. In Charles Borromeo we can also see the essential prerequisite for a similar renewal. Charles could convince others because he himself was a man of conviction. He was able to exist with his certitudes amid the contradictions of his time because he himself lived them. . . . And he could live them because he was a Christian in the deepest sense of the word, in other words, he was totally centered on Christ. What truly counts is to reestablish this all-embracing relation to Christ. No one can be convinced of this all-embracing relationship to Christ through argumentation alone. One can live it, however, and thereby make it credible to others and invite others to share it.

Restoration of the permanent diaconate was resisted in many circles for many reasons. There were some who felt it duplicated what was being done by priests. There were those who feared it was a step backwards to pre-Vatican II clericalism. There were some who reacted negatively due to their own insecurity.

Still, it came about, Christ-centered in its application and name, *diakonia*, service.

Many of those who first supported its restoration during the Vatican Council did so out of concern for the Church in the Third World nations. The diaconate, it was reasoned, would fill the gap of altogether too few priests in the underdeveloped countries that were experiencing increased conversions. The diaconate would allow immediate formation of native men of spirituality and faith, who would relate both to their culture and the teachings of the Church.

This concept of diaconal service has come to pass, but not to the extent first predicted. The most dramatic growth in the ranks of this order has been in the developed, industrialized nations, thus giving support to Cardinal Ratzinger's observation that true restoration moves forward. Those implementing it are people at home in their own times and culture.

Restoration of the permanent diaconate, then, is seen as still continuing. Each passing year sees the application of this order to the ever-changing problems of the day. Each group of candidates preparing for ordination is better, in some way or another, than the previous. The identity of the order does not find itself burdened down with passé perceptions as does the priesthood in the post-conciliar Church. Yet like the priesthood, it takes its identity, value, and empowerment from Jesus Christ who is active in the world today, and who is leading all to the consummation of history.

V.

Discernment

DISCERNMENT, by definition, not only includes perceiving a reality, but also the comprehending of something hidden or obscure. Discernment for the prospective diaconate candidate calls him to comprehend God's will for him. It is not a formula. It is not a technique giving a finite answer. It is a process, and it takes time. It also, and more importantly, takes prayer.

To aid those responding to an apparent call to this order, three methods for spiritual discernment are offered. It is suggested that they each be tried in an unrushed, prayerful fashion. They can be used immediately, and again after one has gathered more information and input on the diaconate. They can, and possibly should be repeated several times throughout the formation process.

a. In Five Steps

Bishop John C. Favalora, of St. Petersburg, Florida, describes a useful discernment process with five steps. While it may not fit the needs of everyone facing such a decision, it does give both the key elements of discernment, and a starting point for those needing one.

[It is very effective. It helped me through both the pre-application days, and when I found myself questioning what I had gotten myself into during a low point in my second year of formation.]

1. THE EXTERNAL DATA:

> Read what there is to read about the question. Find out the particulars, the times, the requirements, the rules, the regulations. Ask questions about the expectations, the pros, the cons, the ups and the downs. With all this information in hand, start compiling information on yourself. Look at yourself, your personal history, your talents, gifts, and shortcomings. Identify the true real you, not the one you present to others, or that "you" they believe is real. Then ask yourself how you are seen in the various roles you live. What are those roles? Come to terms with the reality that is you.

[This may cause mixed feelings about yourself. Don't back off even if some of what you see about yourself is less than perfect. If it's the first time you have seen some of these flaws, chances are those close to you are so used to them that they hardly notice them. They are part of the person your family has come to love.]

2. PRAY:

> Start by being open to the Holy Spirit. Pray for openness to the Holy Spirit. Pray, not so much for this vocation, but to see what God wants you to do. Pray some more, then listen. Give it time.

3. CONSULTATION:

A decision cannot be made in a vacuum. Talk it over with your spouse, children, friends, people in the Church and others who have gone through the same process. Talk to other candidates, to deacons, and priests. Listen to what they all have to say.

4. DECIDE:

No one can make the decision but you. [Some will make this decision quickly and easily. I found it the most right thing I had decided to do since proposing to Barbara. Others will have to work much harder at it.]

5. THE SPLIT DECISION:

If there is an apparent split decision by the time you reach number four, go back and think it out again.

Bishop Favalora says he has only one other suggestion if a person is stuck at number five. He calls it the "Favalora Principle." "Ask yourself if your guts feel at ease with the decision," he says. "Often as not, our body will tell us the truth while our minds and hearts are all confused with lesser concerns. God is our loving Father. He does not want us to suffer needlessly. A prayer asking to be shown His will is one of the most promptly answered prayers."

Some questions Bishop Favalora offers applicants to ask themselves indicate the types of things a person approaching a life of ministry must face.

Do you feel God is calling you?

Why do you feel you want to respond?

Do you see yourself as a sinner?

Are you weak enough to answer?

Do you realize the need for reconciliation?

Are you willing to carry the cross?

b. Discernment For Two

The discernment process for the diaconate in the majority of cases will be done by two people. Not only is the potential candidate called upon to seek out the will of God, his wife must do the same. To aid in the process, and focus it on prayer and scripture, Deacon Thomas Caffery, of New Orleans, has developed the following approach.

He provides prospective applicants with several passages from the Bible, and has the husband ask himself one set of questions, and the wife another. (Of course this doesn't require an unmarried applicant to get a partner just so he can use this method. A single man can use it also.)

First the scriptural passage is listed so that it can be looked up, read, and prayed over. Questions for the husband are on the left, and the questions and considerations for the wife are on the right. The couple should work on their responses separately, writing their ideas down. Then they can discuss their individual responses and feelings. This method of discernment provides an opportunity for honest, open sharing and growth, prerequisites if a couple decides to enter formation.

RUTH 1:1-8

Spiritual discernment is all about the heart! Can I tell my story; when did I (like Ruth) decide to	Am I prepared to follow my husband, wherever his call takes him? Am I prepared to fully sup-

follow God wherever He takes me? Describe that moment in your past when God "touched" you.

port his ministry? Love demands honesty! Guilt has no place in discernment.

1 SAMUEL 3:1-10

Am I "familiar" enough with the Lord to know His voice when I hear it? Is anyone else suggesting to me that the Lord is calling me? Am I listening to the Lord's call, or telling the Lord what I want to hear?

Do I hear the Lord calling my husband? Is the Lord's voice familiar to me? Is He calling me to be the wife of a deacon? How can I help my husband's discernment process?

LUKE 1:26-33 *versus* LUKE 1:5-22

Is my listening (discernment) rooted in faith and trust? Am I open and trusting like Mary or doubting and resisting like Zechariah? Am I trying to control the outcome or am I open to whatever is being asked of me?

Am I listening (discerning) in faith and trust? Am I open like Mary, or resisting like Zechariah? Am I open to whatever is being asked of me?

MARK 2:13-14 *versus* MARK 10:17-31

Am I free to respond to a call like Matthew (Levi) or am I attached like the rich young man? What might my attachments be? Am I attracted to possible attachments of a deacon? (Popularity, powers, pretty vestments?)

Am I free to respond to God's call for me or my husband, or am I attached to something? What are my attachments?

1 CORINTHIANS 12:4-11

What are my gifts and how can I use these gifts for the "common good"? Is becoming a deacon "right" for me at this particular time in my life? Where at this moment in my life is God calling me to use my gifts?

Do I see my husband possessing the gifts of a deacon? Is becoming a deacon "right" for him at this time, or does he have family responsibilities that he should consider? What are my gifts? What ministry should I be involved in at this time in my life?

ACTS 6:1-6

The disciples asked the community to look for men acknowledged to be "deeply spiritual"; they did not look for good workers! Is the community calling me? Is my spirituality recognized at home, in the work place, neighborhood, etc?

Do I see my husband as "deeply spiritual"? How does the community see him? Am I prepared to grow spiritually as he grows spiritually?

JOHN 1:35-39

Discernment (says Thomas Green) is knowing the Lord well enough to "read His face"! Do I understand that the most important goal for me is not "to be or not to be" a deacon, but to grow ever closer to the Lord? Imagine Jesus saying to you personally, "come see!" Spend time with the Lord in order to determine (to read His face) if He is calling you to be a permanent deacon.

Am I comfortable following the Lord close enough to "read His face"? What is He calling me to do? Am I prepared to follow Him?

At this level, discernment not only calls for openness to God, but openness to each other. If either spouse feels the urge not to say everything they think and feel, they should consider the consequences. Holding back from valid feelings and concerns inevitably leads to a weakening of trust.

c. *Ignatian Discernment*

St. Ignatius of Loyola is called upon to provide another approach to spiritual discernment that might be useful to those approaching the diaconate for the first time, and others who are in the middle of formation. (Discernment doesn't end with requesting acceptance into a Permanent Diaconate program. It is an ongoing, vital part of true formation.)

In the briefest form possible, the Ignatian method derived from his Spiritual Exercises consists primarily of:

A) A belief that the Holy Spirit can reveal God's will in this matter.
B) An indifference to all but God's will.
C) A determination to seek what will bring greater glory to God and the Church.
D) A comparison of the advantages and disadvantages of the two alternatives.
E) A tentative decision based on which alternative is more reasonable.
F) Waiting for a confirmatory sign after the tentative decision. (i.e. a sudden turn of events, hearing very favorable comments from the people, acceptance into a formation program, etc.)

This method is deceptively simple. It requires spiritual detachment. Reliance on the Holy Spirit is immediately followed by one's own will, and the expressed will of others. God's will is the goal and the answer. To test understanding of what is perceived as God's will, a tentative decision is (Step E) made to allow for an open acceptance of a sign confirming or rejecting the decision.

Read over the six steps again. Take time to think about each one separately. Create concrete images in your mind from these abstract concepts.

Questions To Ask

Anyone going through discernment, or formation for the permanent diaconate, faces a number of unknowns. There are numerous questions that call out for answers, but there will be none. There will always be at least a little uncertainty, and doubt, and questions for one's self. Try on each question and mentally walk around the room with it.

Am I ready for the permanent diaconate?

Can I handle the three or more years of studies?

If I apply, will they find me unacceptable?

If I apply and am turned down, what do I tell everybody?

If my wife does not agree, won't she feel guilty for stopping me?

What will the kids say?

Won't it put too much pressure on my family at home, at work, and at school?

What will my friends who knew me when I was young say about me now?

Couldn't my boss think that this will interfere with work, or with being available for overtime and special projects?

I don't want to offend my non-Catholic friends and co-workers, so how do I handle that? By keeping it a secret?

I cannot learn all they want deacons to learn. How can I learn all I would have to know? I haven't even read most of the Bible.

Who am I? I'm not worthy of being on the altar. How can I help others when I haven't run my own life all that well?

What would happen if I became a deacon and people found out what types of sins I have committed in the past?

Why me, anyway?

And the list goes on.

Several important points should be remembered when confronted with questions like these.

First, you are not alone. Every concerned man of good conscience has had the same questions and fears. Anyone asking these questions is reacting to the same circumstances and problems as everyone else approaching this life-changing, life-long decision. One is not unique, different, or strange for having these thoughts. As a matter of fact, just the opposite is true.

Second, very few of these questions can be completely answered by anyone other than the person asking them. The man answering God's call cannot justify anything but his own decision. Basing that decision primarily on what others think or feel, or on how one reacts to their approval or disapproval is wrong. As a divinely created person with a free will, each individual has the responsibility to use that free will. This of course does not mean that one should disregard the advice and counsel of those close to them. It means that all their resources and intelligence must be used to make up their own mind.

Third, prayer is necessary. While prayer is recommended for all decisions in life, it is all the more important in those things dealing directly with the Kingdom of God. Pray and listen. Pray not so much for what you think you want, but rather, pray to be shown God's will. Pray openly. Pray from where you are at this point in your life. Present all your questions to Jesus in prayer. Present your fears and concerns in prayer. Pray in thanksgiving for all that you are. Then, pray by listening.

Note: There are many fine books on prayer. One of the best ways to find the one for you is to ask for a recommendation from someone whose spirituality you feel comfortable with. If you are more traditional in expressing your faith, a book written from a more charismatic approach may not be helpful.

e. *For Wives*

Exactly where does the wife of a possible candidate stand in this whole discernment process? What is her role in this? How does all of this affect her?

These are valid questions, ones with many ramifications. A good starting point in answering them is in the way His Holiness, John Paul II describes these ladies. In his address to a gathering of American deacons and their wives in Detroit, September 19, 1987, he called them, "close collaborators in their ministry." Speaking of the important contribution of married deacons, he said, "So intimate is their partnership and unity in the sacrament of marriage, that the Church fittingly requires the wife's consent before her husband can be ordained a permanent deacon (Can. 1031 §2)."

The wife's role is one of support, in a truly emotional, intellectual, and spiritual manner. During discernment that means helping him realize the true Will of God for him, even if that means he should not apply for consideration at this time. In formation, that means growing intellectually and spiritually with her husband. In ministry after ordination, that means supporting and sharing him as he serves the Church. Since they are joined as one person by the sacrament of marriage, discernment involves both spouses. Openness is an absolute necessity for her at this point, both inwardly to the Will of God, and outwardly to her husband. Nothing can be kept back. Fears, concerns, personal reservations, and even desires and aspirations have to be frankly talked about and dealt with in a loving manner.

Canon Law says that a wife's written consent is required before ordination. But most diaconate formation programs will not even accept a candidate's application unless there is a strong indication of the wife's support and agreement. Just as the discernment process continues for the candidate through all of formation, this process also continues for the spouse.

Reservations that were not apparent during the application stage may surface during the training period. The wife must make a concrete decision to support this life-long commitment. She cannot just agree to it because her husband wants it.

There is a tendency in some instances to begin the discernment process with an improper frame of mind, as far as the couple are concerned. A "head of the household" type of mentality is used. Accordingly, since the husband is interested in this venture, the faithful wife goes along with it, without question. This is to be resisted at all costs.

The collaboration referred to by Pope John Paul II calls for two *equal* partners working together to accomplish the same goal. In discernment that means trying to determine the Will of God for him, the husband, for her, the wife, and for them, the married couple.

One of the first things a wife assisting her husband in discernment should do is pray. Only in prayer will she hear the Lord speak in the silence of the heart. Next she should seek out as much information as her husband. That should always include *Permanent Deacons in the United States: Guidelines on Their Formation and Ministry*, by the National Conference of Catholic Bishops, especially Chapter 4. This is the section that deals specifically with married deacons. It discusses the stable marriage and loving family life that contribute to this ministry, participation by the wife in the formation program, the involvement of the entire family, and the Church law prohibiting a married deacon from remarrying if his spouse should die.

There are some considerations that a wife of a candidate should be aware of that do not appear in Church literature. They have to do with both the real and perceived roles a wife is called to fulfill. Others have to do with one's own reactions to these roles, and the incidental events caused by them.

For example, in discernment the wife must not only assist in her husband's discernment for him, but also in her own discernment. She must determine God's will for her, what He is calling her to do, and the manner in which it is to be lived out. Her role may be that of a stabilizing influence as her husband experiences the turmoil caused by resistance to a calling, or the rejection of his application. She may share a new role in their parish community, that of a "wife of a possible diaconate candidate."

Here it is appropriate to acknowledge the reactions of others to his candidacy and/or ordination, because it is the wife who normally is the first to notice changes in attitude. She will observe subtle forms of disapproval or approval in how others react to the idea.

The wife will also begin to experience what one wife called "deacon-wife-itis," the tendency of some people to treat the wife of a deacon differently than before. This might be false expectations of insight or knowledge just because she is married to a deacon, or the applying of a stricter set of standards that the wife is supposed to live by. The erroneous idea here is that deacons and their wives shouldn't react to life's problems the way the rest of humanity does (as if they are now above all that).

Another consideration a wife should be advised of is guilt. It comes in many forms, and for many reasons. A wife could give into the temptation to feel guilty for thinking her husband is not ready to become a candidate, when in fact he really is not. During formation there is possible guilt from not being able to attend all of her husband's classes, even though in fact she has a house to keep up, a job, and children to raise.

There is even a peculiar type of guilt after ordination. It is guilt from being uncomfortable in sharing her husband with God. Yes, even though they are counseled against it, some wives fall prey to this problem. They just cannot seem to justify in their minds that they are a sufficiently important part of their husband's life to have a right to a good part of his time, attention, and affection. To them, their rival is God. So who are they to say "no" to any part of her husband's ministry, no matter how often it takes him away from her or the children.

This brings up the very important ability to say "no." It is this ability, when exercised in love, that keeps things in perspective. It is the ability to say "no," for the right reasons, that allows a couple to grow together, and in the Lord. It is the placing of priorities in one's life, and in one's ministry. (See "ONE, TWO, THREE, in that order")

Up to this point when ministry was discussed it pertained to the man's ministry. Now it is important to focus attention on her ministry.

Let ministry here be understood as service publicly, or at least explicitly designated by the Church to assist in the fulfillment of its mission. Ministry is not the same as mission. Ministry exists for the sake of mission, as a means to that end. Accordingly, any service for the Church is a ministry.

This is pointed out to emphasize that many married women perform outstanding and definite ministries independent of their spouses. Many continue to do so independently of the husband's ministry even after he is ordained. This may be in the form of catechetics, music ministry, formal ministry to the sick or elderly, or informal ministry to those in need of any little help that can be offered.

The discernment process is a time for review of these ministries. It is also a time for a wife to learn what God's will is for her in relationship to her husband's ministry.

That could mean a change from what she was doing to the sharing of his work, or just a ministry of support to one of the Church's ordained ministers, her husband.

This having been said, a caution is offered to the wives of possible candidates: the Church only ordains men (at this time). Regardless of a woman's capabilities, training, and experience in active public ministry, it is the husband who will be evaluated for possible acceptance into the program. Her role will be independent of or complementary to his ordained ministry, but never caused by it. Nor will his ultimate ordination empower her to any independent ministry.

f. Do You Have Permission From Home?

While going through discernment, a man will ask himself many questions. But the above question may not come immediately to mind.

The decision to dedicate one's life, lifestyle, and a fair amount of free time, cannot be made unilaterally. This decision affects more than just the prospective married candidate and his wife. One may not literally need a note from home, but approval, support, or at least acceptance of the idea certainly helps. Getting a reaction from "the kids" is important too.

This reaction may not come immediately. [I still haven't been told by my son Roger what he truly thinks about my ordination. The best I got was "Congratulations. It's pretty good, I guess."] Candidates report surprise as often as a positive or negative response. A smaller number say they were told that it was a surprise that they hadn't applied to the program years before.

The reaction of children can be most interesting and educational. "Children" here refers to those who just barely understand, adolescents, and adult offspring. The reactions are as wide-ranging as the ages. They also give a foretaste of what non-family reactions will be.

The sudden confrontation by children to the idea that their father is somehow going to change can be traumatic. Unfounded fears can cause misplaced or misdirected anger. There can be the fear that dad will not have time to attend their football games or dance recitals. [This is a big one, but one most children don't mention for quite a while.] Some children, due to their level of maturity, will fear what their friends will think of them. Grown children may find this prospect a condemnation of their lifestyle. Both husband and wife should be open to these possibilities, and handle these situations with the grace Christ gives in prayer. Every effort should be made to identify the fears and/or concerns, while trying to see the situation from their perspective, even if it is an ill-formed one.

Some candidates may find themselves faced with so much family approval as to cause a feeling of responsibility to become a deacon. Telling one's family about the applying should not be allowed to cause a popular ordination by acclamation. Family reactions are to be added to the discernment process. They cannot be allowed to replace it.

VI.

Formation

A DEACON CANDIDATE was recently overheard saying, "It wasn't until the middle of the third discernment meeting that I caught on to what formation really meant. But then again, my wife had to explain to me what discernment was."

Formation and discernment are terms not frequently used in many secular circles. Neither word seems to fit into any sports discussion or social interchange. They are very definite in their applications to specialized professions and endeavors. The clergy is one of these professions, even if the diaconate is an unpaid activity for the most part.

The National Conference of Bishops has provided general guidelines for diaconate formation programs. Adequate time is planned for the intellectual and spiritual development of the candidate into the role and office of deacon. That is, in essence, what formation is all about.

Each diocese, facing its own needs and circumstances, establishes its program accordingly. While the Code of Canon Law mandates a minimum of three years for formation, a longer period of time may be required. The bishop decides the length of formation. In the United States there are several models by which formation programs are structured. Some parallel the standard college semesters with weeknight classes. Others have classes every weekend. Still others have extended classroom sessions from Friday evening through Sunday mid-day, once a month.

The one thing required of all formation programs is a fully integrated approach to the formation process. Theological, pastoral, and spiritual considerations must be carefully presented in such a manner that they not only achieve their separate goals, but each supports the other. As the *Guidelines* put it:

> No pastoral practice is likely to be effective if it does not at once derive from sound theological preparation and promote continued theological reflection. Nor is one likely to be a good deacon in Christ's Church if he does not himself live a committed Christian life, with a specifically diaconate spirituality of service. Therefore, the theological, pastoral, and spiritual dimensions of the formation program must be so interrelated that they promote a living integration in the exercise of diaconal ministry. (70)

The *Guidelines*, as was mentioned earlier, devote Chapter 4 to married deacons. Formation programs are to be so structured as to facilitate the wife's involvement. Every effort is to be made to insure that the time spent in formation does not have a negative impact on the couple. The impact of change during formation can only be made positive with understanding of what the candidate is going through.

Take for example theological growth. If the husband and wife start at the same level of education and knowledge, and the wife never takes advantage of the opportunity to learn more, she will find part of their lives not fully shared. It was in all their shared experiences, strains, and struggles that they, as a couple, came to where they were when formation began. That relationship could suffer greatly if one grew in knowledge and the other did not. The same is especially true of spiritual growth.

This does not mean that a candidate's wife has to drop everything — the housework, the children, her job — to sit beside him during each and every class. Her participation should be natural when possible, and excused when it is not. The couple themselves bear much of the burden to make it possible for her to attend classes. The sharing of previously separate roles at home can lead to her being free to share formation. Just realizing and remembering this potential problem has directed many couples to find their own ways to eliminate it.

Another consideration about the overall structure of formation programs is their impact on the candidate's family. Just as the husband and wife can be adversely affected if positive steps are not taken, the rest of the family can be negatively impacted. The children's support can slowly turn into resentment. Their excitement can begin to fade the second or third time classes conflict with something they are doing. The deeper father gets involved in his studies the more likely he is to relate to what they are doing (or not doing) in slightly religious terms, only causing another reason for their displeasure.

They can even become jealous of the faceless names that mother and father keep talking about, the other members of his diaconate class.

Programs realizing this potential problem promote class activities and socials that involve whole families. Again, it is through understanding of the dynamics of this situation that a candidate couple find their own solution.

"Our kids showed their first signs of resentment by complaining about meals," says one candidate's wife. "We both work, so meals on class nights were often rushed. I guess they were right in complaining. I was using leftovers most of the time.

"We finally realized what was happening and came up with a solution. We had a family meeting and discussed what they were feeling. In addition to changing a few things that gave them more of our time, we set class nights as quick food nights. We worked up a schedule; one night hamburgers, another night pizza, another night fried chicken, another roast beef sandwiches. Then we'd repeat the schedule. Either my husband or I would pick up supper on the way home from work. There was less hassle, and more time with the kids."

Three-plus years of preparation can be very taxing on the whole family. This period can also be very rewarding. What makes the difference is what the couple brings to formation, and how they respond to the realities it creates and reveals. Each of the separate years of formation seems to have its own characteristics.

a. First Year

As can be expected, the first year is one of excitement and adaptation. Study skills are learned or relearned. New ways of looking at oneself, the Church, and God are confronted and accepted. Varying levels of confidence and insecurity are faced and dealt with. This first year is also characterized by the establishment of a sense of community.

When people share the same experiences, a bonding takes place. The group takes on a collective personality. Natural support mechanisms develop. Even sub-grouping of similar temperaments and socializing skills takes place. Add to all these natural group dynamics a common goal and a higher ideal, and you produce community.

Each new candidate, his wife, and his family goes through what every other candidate's family goes through. Young or old, high school graduate or Ph.D., all share a common experience and a love of God. They are different in talents and gifts, but they are the same in dedication and goal. This community is not easily explained, but easy to understand when experienced. To some degree the diaconal community typifies the difference between lay ministries and the diaconate. The development of this community is most apparent during the first year of formation.

b. Second Or Middle Year

The second year is often described as the hardest. Not so much for the amount of work and study required, but because of the impact it has on the candidates. For longer programs this may come later, but it is normally experienced around the halfway point in formation. This is a time of questioning. Some formation directors report more withdrawals during this period than any other. The second year, or middle year, has lost the excitement and newness of the first year. It also seems so far from the ordination.

As an indication that this second/middle year does not affect all candidates the same, it is also characterized by remarkable levels of dedication. Some candidates who seemed to be holding back, suddenly blossom. They become involved with the rest of the class activities. They help classmates facing the roller-coaster feelings about their vocation. As one deacon said, "The Holy Spirit seemed to do more work with us that year."

c. Third Or Last Year

The third/last year is also marked by a final coming to terms with God's calling. Such words as "unprepared," "unworthy," and "humbling" are often used by candidates discussing where they are and where they are going. Another trend is the feeling of burnout and impatience. The glowing illusions of what was to come during formation have fallen away. The reality of what a life of ministry calls for is confronted during this time.

[My formation class was particularly affected during our final year by preparations for ordination, not spiritual formation but rather preparation for the ceremony. It became very difficult at times to focus on what was truly important. Committee meetings to decide what music would be used, who would do what, and what the dalmatics and stoles would look like tended to cloud what we were approaching. Individual anxieties often manifested themselves in the inevitable misunderstandings and miscommunications. Wives who had not been able to attend as many classes as they had hoped were especially affected. They didn't understand things the rest of the group had come to terms with much earlier. Our community bond was tested.]

Having said all the above, one fact still remains. Not all formation programs are alike, just as not all candidates are alike. There are similarities in implementation, structure, classes, and evaluations of candidates. It is from the unique resources, needs, and goals of the local church that they each derive their dissimilarities. These differences translate into how each program will impact the candidates during each year of formation. Understanding the dynamics of change experienced during these years can make that impact all the more positive.

d. On Being Formed

Two candidates beginning their third/last year of formation were talking about the coming year. They laughed about all the things they had been directed to read and study that they couldn't remember. They questioned the need for some of the things in the program, and their value in actual ministry.

Finally, one said he had a very interesting realization during a daydream recently.

"I was thinking about how the week before our ordination was going to be. Announcements sent out, cards of congratulations coming in. A number of my relatives would be coming to town.

The house would be filled with activity. We would have a rehearsal that Thursday or Friday before the ordination.

"I pictured all of us kidding around, as we always do. The lot of us nervously going through the motions.

"The night before ordination we would have a dinner for everybody and our families. Then I thought how it would be that Saturday morning, getting up, shaving, getting ready to go to the Cathedral. I could feel the excitement and pride of my wife and kids. I knew I was going to be somehow at peace while feeling I wasn't ready or worthy. You know.

"My family would take pictures and pictures, and afterwards we would go out to eat. The next morning, Sunday, my pastor would have me give one of the homilies. There might even be a little reception for me in the Knights of Columbus Hall after Mass. Then came Monday.

"That's when I realized something about that Monday. That Monday would be just like this past Monday. As a person, I really will be no different come that Monday morning."

The realization of what we are comes to each person in different ways. This candidate suddenly saw his *diakonia*, his servanthood as an unchanged reality. The laying of hands on his head could not change that. The Sacrament of Holy Orders became his outward sign of the graces given all along by Jesus. His formation served to perfect some of that, and his ordination would provide him a life of practice.

The seven sacraments so often serve to make us holy, and increase Christ's loving grace on that which already exists. The desire for salvation and acceptance of Jesus is affirmed in Baptism. Repentance carried into the confessional is rewarded with absolution in Reconciliation. Our longing for union with our redeemer and Savior is fulfilled as we receive Christ in the Eucharist. Human love between a man and a woman is elevated in Matrimony. So too, the response to a calling of service is made holy and empowered in Holy Orders.

Formation, then, is a time of preparation of what already exists. It is true that candidates are taught many things about their religion that they did not know before. They are given an opportunity to nurture and grow in their spirituality. They are given time to mature in their faith and reliance on God. But it is the true self, as loved by the Creator from the first moment of their being, that is prepared for the tasks ahead.

The classroom lectures, the assigned readings, the papers written assist in that preparation. But what each candidate brings to formation will ultimately make him unlike any other deacon ever ordained. If he has openly responded to the calling, putting forth all the effort necessary for full preparation, and has made Jesus the center of all his actions, then that unique deacon will always be aware of the Will of God.

This idea is well documented. The National Association of Permanent Diaconate Directors contracted Selection Research Incorporated (SRI) in 1978 to develop a "Deacon Perceiver Interview." Fr. Patrick McCaslin, founding president of the NAPDD, writes in *Sacrament of Service*:

> Having been involved in the selection, formation, training, evaluation, and call of deacon candidates since 1971, we authors are convinced that we have never "made" a deacon. Deacon talent is either there when training begins, or it will never be there. The Perceiver Interview uncovers clearly in advance whether that talent is or is not there, and is, in our minds, the most significant breakthrough in the discovering and development of deacon talent in America. The reason has to do with the selection process. When a person has the talent to be a deacon, he is a deacon wherever he is. He does not "need" functions, liturgical, sacramental, scriptural, official or unofficial, to BE a deacon. He does not ask "What will I do as a deacon?" He is a deacon, a natural deacon, one who has a deacon nature on which grace can build. The Spirit of God has something special to work with in such a man, namely, a nature that is diaconal and which symbolizes in and for the Church the meaning of diakonia to which it is called.

VII.

Diaconate Formation Programs

THE CATHOLIC CHURCH by its very name is universal. It is the same throughout the world. Yet the very uniquenesses of peoples and ethnic groups calls for a diversity of response to the needs and problems of any given part of the world. It is the local church that ministers to this plurality. A concrete example of this is the variety of ways the restored permanent diaconate has been implemented. The permanent diaconate in the industrialized nations had blossomed beyond first predictions by the Vatican II observers. In Third World nations it has taken on a totally different character, while remaining faithful to the original vision of this order.

Here in the United States there is also evident a diversity in both formation programs and in applications of the permanent diaconate. Each bishop who has sought to establish a program in his diocese, has done so with the unique concerns and circumstances of his pastoral flock in mind. The result is an interesting example of the plurality in the American Catholic Church.

The following are brief descriptions of several permanent diaconate programs from across the country. Each was compiled with the generous help of the diocesan director of that program. By reviewing them one can gain a better appreciation of the similarities and dissimilarities of each program. This should help a prospective candidate understand the formation program in his own diocese.

a. The Archdiocese Of New Orleans

The first program to be described is that of the Archdiocese of New Orleans. It is the one most familiar to the author, since it is the program he attended.

The New Orleans program was established in 1972 by Archbishop Philip M. Hannan, with the first ordinations in 1974. The first class had 19 candidates for the Archdiocese. There have been new classes started every other year since then, providing a staggered schedule of classes. As of the end of 1989 eight groups of candidates have been ordained. There are approximately 150 permanent deacons actively ministering in the Archdiocese.

The selection process for the New Orleans program begins with a notice published soliciting candidate application. Men recommended by their pastor and those personally responding to these announcements are invited to three discernment sessions. These sessions are held over a two month period. Each session features a different topic: "What is a Deacon," "Commitment," and "Individual Discernment." Each session allows time for questions and answers with deacons, their wives, and candidates presently in the program. Applicants and their wives are required to attend all three discernment sessions before the application forms are given out.

These applications ask for the normal personal data: name, address, work experience, educational background, and church participation. Both the applicants and their wives fill out their own application sheets. They are asked separately to tell about themselves, their pastimes, how they exercise their faith, raise their children, and care for themselves. The names and addresses of three references are also requested.

The Archdiocese of New Orleans has no specific educational requirements for diaconate applicants. Still their life and occupational experience should be indicative of an ability to handle the classroom curriculum, and of a faith life that shows spiritual growth and an openness to ministry to others.

Once the application acceptance period is closed, the applicant couples are scheduled for three interviews. These are normally done with a priest, a deacon and his wife, and another priest or deacon. At least one of these interviews is done at the applicant's home, with the whole family present. Reports from these interviews are forwarded to the Permanent Diaconate Advisory Board.

Those completing the three interviews are given a psychological test. The Minnesota Multi-Phasic Personality Inventory (MMPI) is presently being used, as administered by a licensed Clinical Psychologist.

The Advisory Board then meets and reviews each application packet. Their recommendations are forwarded to the Archbishop for final approval. While class sizes are generally between 25 and 30 candidates, the number recommended is primarily governed by the number of apparently qualified candidates among those considered. The two most recent classes had 20 and 32 candidates, respectively.

Selected and deselected applicants and their pastors are contacted and advised of the outcome. Selected candidates are advised via an announcement of a three evening Spiritual Formation program, that takes place the week before their classes begin.

Classes in the New Orleans program are from 7:30 p.m. to 10:00 p.m. Tuesday and Thursday, paralleling the fall and spring college semesters. The first half hour is for either spiritual direction or sharing sessions. Then there are two one hour classes. A Eucharistic celebration is held for the candidates and their wives before class the first Tuesday of each month.

The general curriculum used in this program is as follows.

FIRST YEAR

UNDERSTANDING OLD TESTAMENT LITERATURE

Ancient Near Eastern cultures are examined according to their literary forms; basic concepts. Specific attention to sacred scripture, revelation and inspiration, the canon, text and versions, and textual criticism. Various methods of modern critical interpretation are discussed.

UNDERSTANDING NEW TESTAMENT LITERATURE

A general and specific introduction to the New Testament writings, against the background of their times and an initiation into modern critical methods of interpretation. Emphasis will be placed on personal reading of the text, and progressive acquaintance with both the content and the distinctive religious message of each book.

THEOLOGY OF CHRISTIAN WORSHIP

A study of the nature, history, and fundamentals of liturgy with special emphasis on the Constitution of the Sacred Liturgy of Vatican II: the concepts of worship, sign and symbolism, the relationship between liturgy, scripture and theology.

INTRODUCTION TO SYSTEMATIC THEOLOGY

Theology is the science of faith. It is conscious and methodical explanation and explication of the divine revelation received and grasped in faith. This introductory course studies the divine self-revelation in terms of biblical, personal and historical categories. The student is prepared to appreciate the Vatican II Dogmatic Constitution *Dei Verbum*.

THE CHURCH

The Church is the community of those who confess the Lordship of Jesus Christ, who ratify that faith in Baptism, and who thereby commit themselves to membership and mission within that sacramental community of faith. This course investigates how this community has understood itself and how it has known itself called to collaborate with Jesus' historic mission for the sake of the Kingdom of God.

INTRODUCTION TO SPIRITUAL THEOLOGY

This introductory course indicates means for and stages in the cultivation of a style of life consistent with the presence of the Spirit of the Risen Christ within us and with our status as People of God.

INTRODUCTION TO CHRISTIAN MORALITY

This course emphasizes that the moral life of man is primarily loving response to God's invitation to union with Him rather than a servile obedience to precepts. Grace and virtue are presented as joyful fulfillments of man's natural and supernatural potential.

CHURCH'S MINISTRY OF SERVICE

This course primarily considers the documents of Vatican II. A general background and survey is given in the pre-Vatican II social encyclicals. Reference is also made to the documents of the Puebla Conference and the encyclical *Laborem Exercens*.

SECOND YEAR

OLD TESTAMENT EXEGESIS: THE PENTATEUCH

A verse by verse explanation of the biblical text (Using English translation) of selected passages. Presentation of the results of modern biblical studies (textual) criticism, literary and form criticism, redaction criticism.

NEW TESTAMENT EXEGESIS: THE SYNOPTIC GOSPELS

A comparative study of the first three gospels in the light of Church directed and modern scholarship, illustrating the mission and message of Jesus and the characteristic teaching of each evangelist.

GRACE

The aim of this course is to provide a better understanding of the gifts which God gives us; the implications these gifts have for us as we move and work in our own human world. In addition the course develops ways in which the students speak about God's goodness and gifts in the course of their future apostolic ministries.

SACRAMENTS OF INITIATION

Sacraments of initiation will cover the history and theology of the development of the initiation rites of the Church. Emphasis will be given to the RCIA and its implications in the parish. The history and theology of infant baptism will also be given consideration.

MORAL RESPONSE OF THE CHRISTIAN

This course is sequential to Introduction to Christian Morality and presents man's response to God in the areas of Justice, Fortitude, and Temperance.

CHRISTOLOGY

"Christology" literally means "the word about Christ." This course acquaints the student with the Church's *Traditional* and *Modern* teaching about our Lord, who is true God, true Man, and our brother and leader.

HOMILETICS I (Fall Semester)

HOMELITICS II (Spring Semester)

Introduction to the theology and practice of preaching. The focus of this course is upon models of preparation, the homily outline, delivery, video taping and evaluation of the homily. Students prepare, deliver and critique their work on the Sunday homily.

THIRD YEAR

OLD TESTAMENT EXEGESIS: THE PROPHETS

Introduction to the Prophetic Literature of Hebrew Scripture with selected reading from Amos, Hosea, Micah, Isaiah, and Jeremiah.

NEW TESTAMENT EXEGESIS: THE PAULINE LETTERS

An in-depth exegesis of one of the more important of the Pauline letters, in the context of the Apostle's life and development of his thought, emphasizing major themes and their relevance for today.

INTRODUCTION TO DIACONAL MINISTRY

Practice in preparation and ritual. The course covers the ritual for wake vigil, funeral service, infant baptism, Eucharistic liturgies, para-liturgies, marriage (preparation and ritual), and the practice of the annulment process.

CATECHETICAL METHODS

The principles of catechetics and educational psychology; the history of catechetics in the church as outlined in the NCD; psychological concepts and catechetical methodology; motivation, approaches, needs, discipline, objectives, evaluation and readiness as applied to religious education.

HUMAN SEXUALITY AND MARRIAGE

This course is sequential to the previous courses on morality. It shows that Catholic teaching on love and sexuality is full of joy and hope, made possible by the grace of Christ. It emphasizes the genuinely personalistic emphasis of the church's teaching on sexual ethics.

CANON LAW FOR DEACONS

Introduction to the Code of Canon Law, with emphasis upon the working of the Marriage Tribunal.

HOMILETICS III (Fall Semester)

Thematic homilies: baptism, marriage, funerals.

HOMILETICS IV (Spring Semester)

Homiletics techniques and practice.

SEVENTH SEMESTER

CLINICAL PASTORAL TRAINING

This 13 week course is designed to provide the candidate with basic pastoral skills and understanding of psychology. This is accomplished by weekly lectures, tests, practical experience in pastoral settings, and directed critiques of verbatims recording pastoral encounters.

Candidates are directed to withdraw from all other church related activities so that they can devote their full attention to C.P.T. They are each assigned a formal ministry at which they are expected to give 8 to 10 hours a week of service. These ministries include county prisons, public and private hospitals, and nursing homes. In addition to the small group critique session each week, the candidates meet with an assigned pastoral supervisor. These weekly meetings focus on the candidate, how each is doing, what is happening in their life.

There is an oral exam for each candidate at mid term and again at the end of the course when a written test is given.

[For me C.P.T. (Clinical Pastoral Training) was the culmination and sum total of formation. It gave me an opportunity to use all I had been taught in the preceding three years and what I had brought to formation — a desire to serve Christ by helping others. More importantly C.P.T. allowed me to see myself more clearly.

The person I was 5 years before ever thinking about the diaconate was a different person than the man who applied for acceptance into formation. Likewise I had undergone growth and change as I progressed in the program. Yet on a deeper level I was still the same product of my childhood, of my real and perceived needs, and of my various responses to God's will, both positive and negative. This is the bounty of pastoral counseling.

The two most important lessons I learned during C.P.T. were 1) there is healing power in listening, and 2) it is through understanding my feelings that I am able to help others with what they feel.]

b. The Archdiocese Of San Antonio

The Archdiocese of San Antonio was one of the original 13 dioceses in the United States to begin a permanent diaconate formation program in 1969. The initial class was taught at St. Mary's University as part of their Department of Theology, and was ordained in 1971. The academic qualifications of the program were broadened to include men of dedication and service, but who did not have a higher education background in 1973. The program was lengthened from two to three years in 1977 along with a six month period of supervised internship after academic formation but prior to ordination.

San Antonio now operates two satellite bilingual programs at either end of the Archdiocese in addition to the program at the Oblate School of Theology in San Antonio. They use university staff members and deacons, deacons' wives, and lay instructors.

The Archdiocese of San Antonio's *Permanent Diaconate Guidelines* list the requirements for selections. These norms are very similar to most programs in the United States.

REQUIREMENTS:

a. The applicant must be 35 years of age at the time of ordination. This requirement allows few exceptions made by the Ordinary or the Holy See under specified conditions. He must also be sponsored by a parish or archdiocesan agency. Further, the applicant must understand the possible commitment to celibacy, if single; and if after ordination, he is no longer in the married state.

b. The applicant, if married, must demonstrate evidence of a stable marriage and the enthusiastic support of his wife and family. This requirement is easily fulfilled through letters of recommendation submitted by those who have known the applicant for several years; and home visitation by an ordained deacon and his spouse.

c. The applicant should be in good health. It is required that he have a physical examination within six months of the application date and that a report from the examining physician be submitted to the director.

d. Permanent deacons must be economically stable and self-sufficient. It is expected that the diaconate will be part-time for most permanent deacons, so that each must have a source of income for support of self and family.

e. The applicant should have a history of involvement in the parish or in the community. Evidence of such involvement would be found in the recommendations submitted for the questionnaire completed by the applicant himself. Involvement in parish/community activities not only indicates leadership qualities — desirable in anyone involved in Church ministry — but also an ability to dialogue with others.

f. Graduation from high school or the equivalent is required.

g. Applicants are expected to complete the necessary studies required during the formation period. Credit for theological studies previously completed will not be given except after personal evaluation by the Director and then only for courses pertinent to the diaconate completed within the past five years.

h. The applicant should have a reasonable knowledge of the deacon's role in parish life.

i. Each applicant should have a spiritual and prayerful life prior to entering into the formation and training period. Spirituality should be strengthened while the applicant is in the probationary period of training.

j. A willingness to make a strong commitment of time and talent for study during the three year formation period.

This Archdiocese presently has about 200 permanent deacons serving in parishes, hospitals, and other Archdiocesan programs. The formation program curriculum is described as follows:

The Formation Program desires that candidates demonstrate proficiency in the following areas of theory, information and skill:

a. *Christian Spirituality*: the reality of grace and the life of the Spirit; the nature and history of Christian spirituality; spirituality and ministry; the minister, prayer and spiritual direction; marital spirituality, the Beatitudes and social service ministry.

b. *Theology*: What theology is; how to read theology and engage in theological reflection; the relevance of theology for ministry; the sources of theology in Revelation, tradition and experience; theology as a tool for explaining doctrine and for speculation; the magisterium and the role of theologians; a review of basic Christian doctrines; the history and development of the major themes in Christian theology; essential perspectives of the Second Vatican Council; theology and preaching the Word.

c. *Scripture*: What the Bible is, its history, principal Old and New Testament forms and emphasis; understanding of inspiration; the canon and its composition; basic themes from Scripture; the authority of the Bible; Scripture as a resource for prayer, study, theology and preaching; the Second Vatican Council on the Bible and the contemporary Catholic.

d. *Ecclesiology*: Why a Church — Why this Church; the Second Vatican Council on the Church and its mission in the modern world; history of the images of the Church and their practical implications; initiation and membership; roles, ministries and relationship in the Church; Mary and the Communion of Saints; history of ecumenism and principles of ecumenical dialogue; introduction to the major non-Catholic and non-Christian bodies represented in the territory of the Archdiocese (familiarity with their terminologies, systems of belief, the status of ecumenical dialogue, the possibilities of pastoral cooperation and of sharing).

e. *Liturgy and Sacraments*: Sign, symbol and ritual in a community; the principles of Christian sacramental theology; history of the liturgical reform, particularly the main achievements of the Second Vatican Council; principles of liturgical celebration; roles and ministries in liturgy; the Mass as a community prayer; the Liturgy of the Hours (for group or private prayer, public celebration); review of the Sacraments and relevant Archdiocesan guidelines for their celebration; general perspectives on art, architecture and music in the liturgy; study of the diaconal rites and liturgical functions (with video-taped practice sessions).

f. *Christian Ethics and Social Justice*: The Gospels and the Christian mission; Catholic moral perspective — the obligations of love and law, formation of conscience, magisterium and moral teaching, sin and forgiveness; special questions from pastoral ministry (health care, economic and political ethics, marriage and family); the Church as an agent of change for justice (global issues and local responsibility); strategies and dynamics of Christian social action; basic documentation of Catholic social theory (papal social encyclicals, Second Vatican Council, American Bishops' pastoral statements).

g. *Church History*: The Church as a community in time; the progress of evangelization: major themes, movements, periods and cultural characteristics; changing patterns of evangelization today; review of basic facts, dates, personalities of Church history and their continuing impact; the Catholic Church in the United States, its history, diversity, and role in the world-wide Church today and tomorrow; history of the Archdiocese of San Antonio, factors in its growth, its diversity and potential directions for the future.

h. *Church Structure and Administration*: basic terminology and organizational chart; collegiality and accountability in Church structures at the universal, national, diocesan and parish levels; basic consideration of Canon law; church records; lines of authority, responsibility and communication; the deacon in relation to other ministers and faithful.

i. *Identity of the local Church*: Mission Statement of the Archdiocese of San Antonio; review of major policies of pastoral care, personnel distribution and due process; the history and role of the Archdiocese Directory; the demography, area profiles and projections for the Archdiocese; Archdiocesan resources and public services available for pastoral care.

j. *Homiletics*: The nature of diaconal preaching (extent of the faculty to preach, preaching as ministry and within ministry);

types of preaching (homily, sermon, speech); imagery and story-telling; organization and preparation; use of Scripture and theology; the Lectionary as resource and norm; physical dynamics of public speaking (technique, delivery, style); preaching for special audiences; speech therapy and coaching, with evaluation; practice homilies (with video-tape critique session).

After satisfactorily completing the 3 year academic formation program, candidates go through a 6 month supervised internship prior to ordination. The Archdiocese of San Antonio's *Permanent Diaconate Guidelines* describes this internship as follows:

1. At the conclusion of the basic academic and skill training components, the Program will require of each candidate for ordination a formal period of Internship. The purpose of this Internship is to meet several objectives:

   A. it will allow the candidate to consider the commitment of ordination in an atmosphere of greater freedom and objectivity;

   B. it will help to discourage the identifying of ordination with completion of the Formation Program;

   C. it will give the candidate a more authentic experience of typical patterns of diaconal service, unencumbered by regular attendance at classes and formation sessions, so that he may evaluate the likely effects on his family and job responsibilities before making a final commitment;

   D. it will afford a better opportunity to structured observation and evaluation of a candidate in more realistic circumstances, and so will help the Program and the candidate to judge more accurately his probable success in an actual ministerial role;

   E. it will provide time for a more flexible course of liturgical and homiletic practice-sessions;

2. The following terms will apply to the Internship for deacon-candidates. Internship will be mandatory for all candidates, upon satisfactory completion of required academic and skill training components. The Internship will be under the direction of the Program, which continues to be responsible for the candidate and his development. The Internship site will be a parish, agency, institution, or apostolate offering good possibilities for supervised experience in a three-fold ministry of charity, the Word and liturgy.

3. The details of the Internship Agreement will be negotiated by the Program, with the personnel of a selected site and the individual candidate and his spouse. The Program will provide clear guidelines regarding supervision, which will be the chief responsibility of Internship site personnel; regular contact will be maintained between the Internship supervisor and the Program. The intern will receive no financial remuneration from the Internship site except for reimbursement of out-of-pocket expenses incurred in the course of assigned duties. Upon reasonable request of either party to it, provisions of the Internship Agreement may be adjusted subsequently, with the approval of the Director.

4. Internship will begin at the conclusion of the educational and skill training components. The duration of the Internship will be, at a minimum, six months; renewal of the Internship Agreement may be elected by the candidate or recommended by the Program staff upon evaluation of the candidate's intern experience and consideration of all circumstances. The Internship may be extended to a maximum of two years, at the end of which time the Program may 1) ask for a definite commitment from the candidate to seek ordination; 2) recommend an indefinite leave of absence; 3) recommend withdrawal from

the program. Upon satisfactory completion of an Internship Agreement and with the final endorsement of the Program, a candidate may present a petition for ordination to the diaconate.

5. The intern experience must help the candidate to evaluate objectively his ministerial skills and his ability to integrate successfully the responsibilities of family, job and ministry. Of critical importance is the role of the on-site supervisor, who will need to balance personal concern of the candidate with objective detachment in the interest of promoting good ministerial performance.

6. Of key importance in judging the value of the Internship will be evidence of the candidate's attitude. He should demonstrate openness to learning from the experience, both objectively and subjectively. Any impatience with the process (as distinct from specific episodes) should be probed, to be sure that eagerness for ordination does not get in the way of real growth in ministerial ability. Care must be taken lest the Internship be regarded as an artificial requirement for Orders.

7. The Program will rely on the consistency of good reports on the candidate's intern performance, from the on-site supervisor and other personnel; and on the honesty and completeness of the candidate's own evaluation of how his experience in the Internship has helped him to discern whether he should accept a call to ordination. Particular attention will be paid to the candidate's judgment of the mutual relation of his ministry and his family and job responsibilities and, in the case of a married candidate, to the congruence of his judgment with that of his wife.

c. Formation For The Local Church

The general elements of the New Orleans and San Antonio formation programs are typical of the majority of the 155 programs in the United States. Some may use a different sequence of classes or have a different emphasis each year, but the basics are the same. They have been developed from the collective trials and errors of almost 20 years' experience.

Some of the unique elements found in individual programs are caused by such things as geography, cultural needs, and pastoral priorities. Eleven dioceses in the South and Southwest operate both English and Spanish speaking formation programs. Brownsville, Texas, for example has a population that is 85% Catholic and of these 90% are Hispanic. To serve, deacons must be able to communicate. The Diocese of Fort Worth addresses this problem in another way. They operate an English speaking program, but all candidates must learn enough Spanish to proclaim the Word.

Another cultural adaptation is found in South Dakota. Fr. John Hatcher, SJ, has developed a whole formation program around the pastoral, social, and traditional concerns of Native Americans. Nationally there is even a growing Native American Deacons Association with over 100 deacons and candidates.

The vast expanses of the Diocese of Fairbanks, Alaska, have not stifled the growth of the permanent diaconate. Fr. Rene Astruc, SJ, has put together formation materials for the Yup'ik Eskimo tribes. He is often flown to a central village by his pilot/Bishop Michael J. Kaniecki, SJ, where candidates in formation come from their outlying villages for instruction. Sometimes he has to go by snowmobile, presenting a modular formation program. While most programs use the traditional classroom setting, the Alaskan classes are more frequently held around a woodstove in someone's home.

Size also has its impact on formation programs. While Fairbanks has 35 permanent deacons, Washington, D.C., has 164, and Boston has 140. The largest diaconate program is in Chicago. The second largest program has 200+ deacons, while Chicago has over 600 active permanent deacons.

Still another consideration is the educational requirements of individual programs. The majority require a high school diploma. A few have no minimum educational requirements, and others require a college degree. The Archdiocese of Portland, Oregon, is evaluating a proposal to require all candidates to have completed some postgraduate study.

The United States Catholic Conference Committee on the Permanent Diaconate survey of deacons (Oct. 31, 1989) reveals a wide range of educational backgrounds. Of the 9,400+ permanent deacons 4% have an 8th grade education or less, 28% have graduated from high school, 23% have some college, and 28% have an undergraduate degree. 1,600, or 18% of deacons have completed some graduate work, or have their Masters or Doctorate.

Scheduling of classes sets some programs apart from others. Most use the college schedule of fall and spring semesters of weekly or bi-weekly classes. Others have monthly sessions. Honolulu, Alaska, and more urban areas like Fort Worth have formation sessions 10 weekends a year with required reading and reports in between. Even Washington, D.C., which has weekly classes, uses Saturday workshops once a month.

The Bishops' *Guidelines* establish a minimum of three years for formation, but the national average is now closer to four and a half years. Some dioceses are presently linking their lay ministry formation programs to diaconate programs. In these areas the applicant must first complete the two to three years of lay ministry training to be qualified for acceptance into the diaconate program of another two to three years.

VIII.

Canon Law And The Permanent Diaconate

IT IS INTERESTING to note that during the period between the end of the Second Vatican Council and Pope Paul VI's encyclical *Ad Pacendum* setting forth the norms for the permanent diaconate, the Vatican was rewriting Canon Law. One did not cause the other to happen, but the new Code certainly clarified many issues pertaining to the diaconate. Restoration of the permanent diaconate would have been more difficult and confusing had the Code not been revised. The very time frame in which the old Code of Canon Law was drafted was light years removed from much of the post-conciliar Church thinking. Last revised in 1917, Canon Law, the set of rules for governing the Church, has undergone some interesting changes.

These changes were promulgated by Pope John Paul II in January of 1983. They incorporate both the intent of the Council Fathers relative to the permanent diaconate, as well as several things learned during the first years of restoration. Specified canons pertaining to the permanent diaconate rely heavily on the canonical norms written by Pope Paul VI in *Sacrum Diaconatur Ordinem* as well as *Ad Pascendum.*

Since one of the goals of this book is to present, in one place, as many valuable resources presently available lending understanding to the diaconate, a review of 40 related Canons is presented. Where it will shed some light on a particular facet of this order, or be of comparative interest, related, but outdated canons from the 1917 code are mentioned. For purposes of order, the canons will be presented in their sequence rather than by topic.

CANON 194

§*1*. ***One is removed from an ecclesiastical office by the law itself:***
- ***1° who has lost the clerical state;***
- ***2° who has publicly defected from the Catholic faith or from the communion of the Church;***
- ***3° a cleric who has attempted marriage even if only civilly.***

§*2*. ***The removal from office referred to in nn.2 and 3 can be enforced only if it is established by the declaration of a competent authority.***

This canon is binding on all clerics, and that of course includes deacons. Paragraph 1, no. 3 relates directly to the prohibition against remarriage by permanent deacons should their wife die, Canon 1087. In simple terms, a deacon getting married is no longer a deacon. He is removed.

There are canonical provisions by which the pope can waive the remarriage prohibition. But these matters are based on individual circumstances and may not be easily appreciated in limited general discussions.

CANON 213

The Christian faithful have the right to receive assistance from the sacred pastors out of the spiritual good of the Church, especially the word of God and the Sacraments.

Herein lies the basic obligation of ministry for all in the clerical state. As ministers of the Word and the Eucharist, deacons are compelled to serve the faithful. They are not to be ordained for themselves. They are not ordained as a reward for holiness or good deeds. They are ordained to minister to the faithful. The people of God not only have a right to the sacramental goods of the Church, but also to available ministers, effective liturgy and preaching that opens the Scriptures and relates to real life.

CANON 236

According to the prescription of the conference of bishops, aspirants to the permanent diaconate are to be formed to nourish a spiritual life and instructed in the correct fulfillment of the duties proper to this order in the following manner:

1° Young men are to live for at least three years in some special house unless the diocesan bishop decides otherwise for serious reasons;

2° Men of more mature age, whether celibate or married are to spend three years in a program determined by the conference of bishops.

This canon deals with two age groups, one of younger years, and the other of a more mature age. General legislation of the church allows for 25 year old deacons. The United States Conference of Bishops opted for a 35 year old minimum age for the ordination of permanent deacons, eliminating the need for a "special house" and the restrictions this would place on those seeking the order. The three year formation period was also adopted by the United States Bishops. It is often looked upon by those in formation as a symbolic parallel to the time spent by Christ's disciples during His years of public ministry. [Those of a Protestant background will see this rule as a major difference with the elected or appointed deacons of some denominations.]

CANON 266

§*1*. *A person becomes a cleric through the reception of diaconate and is incardinated into the particular church or personal prelature for whose service he has been advanced.*

Permanent deacons are not part of the laity. Ordination makes them clerics. Ordination also attaches them to the particular church, the diocese, they are chosen to serve. [This canon is also a reason the term "lay deacons" should never be used to describe deacons in the Catholic Church. It is a conflict in terms.]

As clerics, deacons are bound by several other specific canons: Canons 273, 274, and 275 are among these. Canon 273 calls for reverence and obedience to the pope and the ordinary, the bishop, by all clerics. Canon 274 similarly requires clerics to accept the assignments given them by their bishop. Canon 275 binds all clerics in a common bond of fraternity, and directs them toward the mission of the laity.

CANON 276

§*1*. *In leading their lives clerics are especially bound to pursue holiness because they are consecrated to God by a new title in their reception of orders as dispensers of God's mysteries in the service of His people.*

§2. *In order for them to pursue this perfection:*

- ***1° first of all they are faithfully and untiringly to fulfill the duties of pastoral ministry;***
- ***2° they are to nourish their spiritual life from the two-fold table of Sacred Scripture and the Eucharist; priests are therefore earnestly invited to offer the sacrifice of the Eucharist daily and deacons are earnestly invited to participate daily in offering it;***

3° priests as well as deacons aspiring to the priesthood are obliged to fulfill the liturgy of the hours daily in accordance with the proper and approved liturgical books; permanent deacons, however, are to do the same to the extent it is determined by the conference of bishops;

4° they are also bound to make a retreat according to the prescriptions of particular law;

5° they are to be conscientious in devoting time regularly to mental prayer, in approaching the sacrament of penance frequently, in cultivating special devotion to the Virgin Mother of God, and in using other common and particular means for their sanctification.

This particular canon focuses directly on the holiness of life that all clerics, including permanent deacons, must strive toward. It gives a means for achieving that perfection in five parts. While this is an updated rule from the 1917 Canon Law which dealt only with priests and transitional deacons, it now covers the needs of the permanent deacon. It is notably less specific in its guidelines than the 1917 version.

After firmly establishing the obligation to strive toward holiness, this canon first requires a deacon to "faithfully and untiringly" do what he was ordained to do, this is, pastoral ministry to the People of God in service. This is a serious obligation. It not only speaks to the functional, operational, administrative, and spiritual needs of the faithful, but it addresses a fundamental means by which the deacon can achieve his own holiness. Only then does this canon deal with his spiritual life.

The second puts forth Sacred Scripture and the Eucharist as two primary sources of spiritual nourishment. Scripture allows us to learn about God's will, and at the same time provides an opportunity for Him to speak to our hearts. As preachers of the Word deacons must first meditate on the Scriptures and make it truly part of their lives. The Eucharist should be received as often as possible.

The earnest invitation to priests to say Mass daily replaces a canonical mandate to do so found in the old Code. The private Mass is de-emphasized with a fuller understanding of this celebration as communal. Priests are now encouraged to say daily Mass, and deacons are encouraged to participate in offering it. There are local circumstances that keep both priests and deacons from fully responding to this recommendation, as there are circumstances limiting deacons from participating in every Mass they attend. A deacon in a pew with his whole family can be as catechetical as any homily he could give on the importance of the family.

The one firm obligation this canon mandates for all clergy is the recitation of the daily Divine Office. The Liturgy of the Hours is described as an "ancient tradition and immemorial custom," and is capable of becoming a framework around which one can build a strong prayer life. Once referred to as the priest's Breviary, this book of psalms, prayers, and scriptural readings for different parts of the day is now required of priests and transitional deacons. The United States Bishops' Committee on the Permanent Diaconate spells out the rule under this canon for American permanent deacons: "The deacon can very appropriately pray the liturgical hours of Lauds and Vespers as expressing the praise of God from the entire church community." In other words a deacon should recite at least one part of the Liturgy of the Hours each day, as his lifestyle permits. [Sadly, in some places it is not easy to find a deacon who can tell you what week it is in the Liturgy of the Hours.]

Retreats, every year or two, are also made obligatory for all clerics by this canon. The application of this rule is still at the discretion of the local bishop and can take the form of retreats in common or individual structured retreats, and may include days of recollection. The goal is always the same. Time must be set aside for the ordained person to withdraw from day to day ministry and minister to his own spiritual health. It is the holiness of life that is the object of this whole canon.

Finally, Canon 276 recommends common practices of piety. The 1917 canon placed the responsibility on the bishop to see what religious practices were carried out. The 1983 Code puts the responsibility on each cleric. In this case, on each deacon. Just as the laity are called upon to be more involved in their salvation, clerics are also. Gone are the rigid rules on how often confession was required, etc.

Regular mental prayer, frequent reception of the sacrament of Reconciliation, and special devotions to the Virgin Mary are now encouraged. How they are made part of a deacon's, or deacon candidate's life marks this strength in growth towards holiness. [It is very tempting for a deacon, or anyone in ministry to get so involved with "doing" that they neglect their constant spiritual growth. Praying is more important than doing.]

CANON 277

§***1.*** ***Clerics are obliged to observe perfect and perpetual continence for the sake of the kingdom of heaven and therefore are oblidged to observe celibacy, which is a special gift of God, by which sacred ministers can adhere more easily to Christ with an undivided heart and can more freely dedicate themselves to the service of God and humankind.***

§***2.*** ***Clerics are to conduct themselves with due prudence in associating with persons whose company could endanger their obligation to observe continence or could cause scandal for the faithful.***

§***3.*** ***The diocesan bishop has the competence to issue more specific norms concerning this matter and to pass judgment in particular cases concerning the observance of this obligation.***

Celibacy for clerics in the West finds its roots in the first three hundred years of the Church. The 1983 Code confirms the same basic tenets as earlier Church law, but does so in light of a clearer, more positive understanding of this gift. The emphasis on the goal of celibacy as a symbol of the essence of the ministry takes its justification from theology and spirituality.

The Second Vatican Council reaffirmed its commitment to this feature of priestly life. Accordingly, celibacy was linked to the ministry of the re-established permanent diaconate, although in a modified form. While it is held to be a highly esteemed gift, celibacy is not promoted by the Church as an essential requirement of priesthood and/or of diaconal ministry. A fuller discussion of these ideas can be found in Article 16 of *Presbyterorum Ordinis*. The latter part of this Article addresses obligatory celibacy in priests:

> This sacred Council approves and confirms this legislation so far as it concerns those destined for the priesthood, and feels confident in the Spirit that the gift of celibacy, so appropriate to the priesthood of the New Testament, is liberally granted by the Father provided those who share Christ's priesthood through the sacrament of Orders, and indeed the whole Church, ask for the gift humbly and earnestly.

Gone from the canon and from its official commentary is the supposed need for "cultic purity," a concept that indirectly depreciated the body and sexuality. The 1917 canon had this negative motive for celibacy, proscribing violations of it as sacrilege.

Two ancient canons are of curious interest and display some of the limited perspectives within the early Church that led to the 1917 Code. The Council of Elvira, 305 A.D. wrote as their Canon 33:

> Let bishops, priests, and deacons, and in general all the clergy who are specially employed in the service of the altar, abstain from conjugal intercourse with their wives and the begetting of children. Let those who persist be degraded from the ranks of clergy.

It was the Council of Rome, in 386 A.D., that wrote Canon 9:

> We advise that priests and deacons should not live with their wives.

Those familiar with the heresy of Manichaeism will understand what that school of thought said about the human body and sexuality, and how it affected even the mainstream of Catholic thought. There are many similar negative perspectives that have lingered on through the centuries that only found their defeat with Vatican II. The positive reasons for celibacy, that cannot be explained purely theoretically, are being given an opportunity to be lived out in faith.

CANON 278

§*1*. *Secular clerics have the right to associate with others for the purpose of pursuing ends which befit the clerical state.*

§2. *Secular clerics are to place great value upon those associations in particular which, having statutes recognized by the competent authority, foster holiness in exercise of the ministry by means of a suitable and properly approved style of life and by means of fraternal assistance, and which promote the unity of the clergy among themselves and with their own bishop.*

§*3*. *Clerics are to refrain from establishing or participating in associations whose ends or activity cannot be reconciled with the diligent fulfillment of the duty entrusted to them by competent ecclesiastical authority.*

As with all the selected canons reviewed here, this one specifically affects deacons. The impetus for this right is found in the very social nature of all mankind, and the basic rights of all Christians as elaborated in the Vatican II documents. Support for it is described in paragraph 8 of *Presbyterorum Ordinis*.

The specific forming of "unions" that turn clerical ministry into a type of profession is one of the reasons for the third paragraph of this canon. It was as late as 1983 that the decision was made to allow local ordinaries to permit clerics to become members of Rotary Clubs. This permission is not granted for membership in Masonic organizations.

For the permanent deacon in modern American society, Canon 278 requires a judgment about the aims of any organization he would belong to. The general rule of thumb is, if the organization and its standing in the community is compatible with the ministerial obligations of a deacon it is alright for him to be a member. [One of the most timely issues to affect one's membership in an organization is abortion. There are clubs, groups, and even national labor unions coming out in public support for legalized abortion. Such a stand should cause a deacon candidate to reassess his continued membership in such an organization.]

CANON 280

Some community of life is highly recommended to clerics; wherever such a practice exists, it is to be preserved to the extent possible.

This canon primarily documents the Church's strong interest and concern for the community life of priests. While not being as structured as similar canons in previous Codes it still aims at the needs for common support and spiritual assistance now centered around rectory life.

For the permanent deacon, it is a call to be a part of this process where appropriate.

CANON 281

§*1*. ***When clerics dedicate themselves to the ecclesiastical ministry they deserve a remuneration which is consistent with their condition in accord with the nature of their responsibilities and with the conditions of time and place; this remuneration should enable them to provide for the needs of their own life and for the equitable payment of those whose services they need.***

§2. ***Provision is likewise to be made so that they possess that social assistance by which their needs are suitably provided for if they suffer from illness, incapacity or old age.***

§*3*. ***Married deacons who dedicate themselves completely to the ecclesiastical ministry deserve a remuneration by which they can provide for their own support and that of their families; married deacons, however, who receive remuneration by reason of a civil profession which they exercise or have exercised are to take care of their own and their family's needs from the incomes derived from their profession.***

This canon, by and large, is self-explanatory. Priests in full service to the Church are to receive a salary commensurate with their basic needs. This is to include health care.

Married deacons fall into two categories under this rule. 1) Those in full-time ministry who are to be paid by the Church a salary that will allow them to support themselves and their family. 2) Those performing part-time ministry who have a secular occupation or pension.

Permanent Deacons in the United States: Guidelines on Their Formation and Ministry addressed both of these cases in more detail, noting that even part-time deacons should be compensated for expenses incurred in their ministry. Some dioceses arrange for payment of part-time work performed by deacons by using contracts. This is often done to eliminate the need for the deacon to get a second secular job to support his family, and to maximize his usefulness and effectiveness in the local church. (See *Guidelines*, no. 156-159)

Applying paragraph two of this canon to the unique situation and status of deacons would require Church support of those under severe circumstances caused by old age, catastrophic illness, and the like. This subject is of critical interest in many dioceses at this time. The issue of financial liability for permanent deacons has yet to be fully resolved. It is described by some as the most crucial issue facing the permanent diaconate today.

CANON 282

§*1*. ***Clerics are to cultivate a simple style of life and are to avoid whatever has a semblance of vanity.***

§*2*. ***After they have provided for their own decent support and for the fulfillment of all the duties of their state of life from the goods which they receive on the occasion of exercising an ecclesiastical office, clerics should want to use any superfluous goods for the good of the Church and for works of charity.***

As with most of the canons that apply to the clergy, Canon 282 is primarily concerned with priests and bishops. This is especially true in paragraph two, which refers to the "stole fee" or remuneration received for fulfilling some parochial function, such as performing a wedding or baptism. (See Canon 531)

Nevertheless, the call to live a lifestyle that is not antagonizing to the poor is made to deacons as well as priests. While this does not ask the successful businessman who becomes a deacon to sell his belongings, second car, four bedroom house and Rolex watch, and move into a rented efficiency apartment, pastoral sensitivity is urged. How one uses that which he has been graced determines the simplicity of his lifestyle, not the quantity of those graces.

CANON 283

§*1*. ***Even if they do not have a residential office, clerics nevertheless are not to leave their diocese for a notable period of time, to be determined by particular law, without at least the presumed permission of their proper ordinary.***

§2. ***Clerics are entitled to a due and sufficient period of vacation each year, to be determined by universal or particular law.***

Attention is brought back to the primary fact that a man is ordained for the good of the diocese, the local church. Accordingly, absence from the local church must be approved, at least with presumed permission. Since the general norm is a one month annual vacation, presumed permission is expected for that duration of time. Time spent on retreat is not included in these 30 days, which can be spread over several intervals.

Deacons assigned to a parish or other ministry would normally notify their normal superior, the pastor, or program director. Deacon/pastors generally make notification through their Chancery. Deacons not assigned to full-time ministry do, of course, experience the need to be absent from their diocese because of professional requirements or family situations. These are handled on an individual basis in most dioceses through normal channels.

CANON 284

Clerics are to wear suitable ecclesiastical garb in accord with the norms issued by the conference of bishops and in accord with legitimate local custom.

While it is interesting to read all the historical notations and comments on clerical garb for priests, the intent here is to relate this canon to the permanent deacon. The *Guidelines*, paragraph 130, give the best explanation.

> The Code of Canon Law (Canon 288) exempts permanent deacons from the obligation of wearing ecclesiastical garb. However, in exceptional circumstances, a diocesan bishop, with due consideration, may decide that deacons should wear some distinctive garb when engaged in formal clerical ministry. For liturgical services, of course, the rubrical vestment is required.

Although the roman collar was widely used by deacons during the first years of restoration in this country, this is no longer the case. The practice not only caused numerous cases of mistaken identity, but gave those resisting the restoration a focal point for criticism. One example for limited permission to wear the roman collar: a deacon assigned as chaplain to a police agency where he assists in hostage negotiations. [Some years ago, a permanent deacon wearing a roman collar during a hospital visit was grabbed by a man running down the hall. All the man said was ''come with me, my mother is dying.'' At the man's mother's room the deacon had to explain he wasn't a priest and could not anoint the woman or give her absolution. The family, in their state of distress, could not be made to understand.]

CANON 288

Permanent deacons are not bound by the prescriptions of Canon 284, 285, §§3 and 4, 286, 287, §2, unless particular law determines therwise.

To facilitate this review of canons relevant to the diaconate, Canons 285, 286 and 287 will be covered in a further review of Canon 288. The preceding canon limits the activity of the clergy.

Canon 288 releases permanent deacons from most of these limitations.

Priests are prohibited from holding public office under Canon 285, as well as from managing civil property or funds, or having secular offices which require financial accountability. Deacons are not so limited.

Priests are not to take active part in political parties, or lead labor unions under Canon 287. Deacons are not so prohibited. Canon 287 starts off, first, by saying that clerics are always to foster that peace and harmony based on justice which is to be observed among all persons. Deacons are bound to uphold this part of the canon. [While deacons can hold public office, most bishops ask to be notified if one of their deacons plans to run for office. The issue of abortion legislation, and moral/legal matters must be sensitively addressed.]

CANON 517

§*1*. ***When circumstances require it, the pastoral care of a parish or of several parishes together can be entrusted to a team of several priests in solidum with the requirement, however, that one of them should be moderator in exercising pastoral care, that is, he should direct their combined activity and answer for it to the bishop.***

§*2*. ***If the diocesan bishop should decide that due to a dearth of priests a participation in the exercise of the pastoral care of a parish is to be entrusted to a deacon or to some other person who is not a priest or to a community of persons, he is to appoint some priest endowed with the powers and faculties of a pastor to supervise the pastoral care.***

Unfortunately, the poor response to priestly vocations has caused this canon to be used in many areas of the country. It makes provision for the operation, both administratively and pastorally, of an otherwise "priestless parish." It also makes provision for a deacon, lay religious, or community of lay religious to be entrusted with the cares of such a parish. The effectiveness of this practice, although successful in a number of current cases, is still being analyzed.

CANON 757

It is proper for presbyters who are co-workers with the bishops to proclaim the gospel of God; pastors and others entrusted with the care of souls are especially bound to this office as regards to the people entrusted to them; deacons also are to serve the people of God in the ministry of the word in communion with the bishop and his presbyterate.

This canon clearly spells out the grave duty and responsibility to preach the gospel message for priests and deacons. The difference is one of faculty inherent to the priesthood, but rendered to the deacon based on talent and training. This means that even though a deacon is authorized canonically to preach the Gospel, he does so only in communion with the bishop and his presbyterate. Accordingly, if an individual deacon does not exhibit this talent and fails to respond to appropriate training, he may not be given this faculty by the bishop. [Ironically, deacons who wish to preach must prove themselves. Priests who are bad preachers have to prove nothing, and are often the ones who decide what Sundays their deacons can preach.]

CANON 762

Since the people of God are first brought together by the word of the living God, which it is altogether proper to require from the mouth of the priest, sacred ministers are to value greatly the task of preaching since among their principal duties is the proclaiming of the Gospel of God to all.

"Sacred ministers" here include deacons. The main thrust of the canon is to emphasize the importance of preaching as a principal duty.

CANON 764

With due regard for the prescriptions of Canon 765, presbyters and deacons possess the faculty to preach everywhere, to be exercised with at least the presumed consent of the rector of the church, unless that faculty has been restricted or taken away by the competent ordinary or unless express permission is required by particular law.

Here priests and deacons are given the faculty to preach anywhere in the world, except when 1) they have had their faculties limited by their bishop, 2) local church legislation prohibits it without permission, 3) the local rector or pastor refuses permission, or 4) permission is necessary from the appropriate religious superior as referred to in Canon 765.

CANON 767

§*1*. ***Among the forms of preaching the homily is preeminent; it is a part of the liturgy itself and is reserved to a priest or a deacon; in the homily the mysteries of faith and the norms of Christian living are to be expounded from the sacred text throughout the course of the liturgical year.***

§*2*. ***Whenever a congregation is present a homily is to be given at all Sunday Masses and at Masses celebrated on holy days of obligation; it cannot be omitted without serious reason.***

§*3*. ***If a sufficient number of people are present it is strongly recommended that a homily also be given at Masses celebrated during the week, especially during Advent or Lent or on the occasion of some feast day or time of mourning.***

§4. ***It is the duty of the pastor or the rector of a church to see to it that these prescriptions are conscientiously observed.***

The lowly ''Sunday sermon'' is here elevated to a position of preeminence. The homily is the primary way in which the faithful will be educated in their faith and spiritually nourished. The homily is not to be omitted without serious reason. While a duly deputized lay person can give a Gospel reflection at a Mass, or preach outside of Mass, the homily, as part of the liturgy, is reserved to priests and deacons.

CANON 831

§*1*. ***Without a just and reasonable cause the Christian faithful are not to write anything for newspapers, magazines, or periodicals which are accustomed to attack openly the Catholic religion or good morals; clerics and members of religious institutes are to do so only with the permission of the local ordinary.***

§2. ***It is the responsibility of the conference of bishops to establish norms concerning the requirements for clerics and members of religious institutes to take part in radio or television programs which deal with questions concerning Catholic teaching or morals.***

This canon codifies common sense. Without just cause we should not aid the enemies of the Church. While lay persons may use their own good judgment as to what that just cause might be, clerics must obtain permission from their bishop before writing.

CANON 861

§*1*. ***The ordinary minister of baptism is a bishop, presbyter, or deacon, with due regard for the prescription of Canon 530, n. 1.***

§2. ***If the ordinary minister is absent or impeded, a catechist or other person deputed for this function by the local ordinary confers baptism licitly as does any person with the right intention in case of necessity; shepherds of souls, especially the pastor, are to be concerned that the faithful be instructed in the correct manner of baptizing.***

Canon 861 updates the Code of 1917 by specifically responding to the restoration of the permanent diaconate. Deacons are ordinary ministers of Baptism. It goes on to identify the extraordinary ministers of this sacrament, both by deputation by the bishop and in emergency situations. Baptismal instruction is not optional; it is required by this canon. [Married deacons bring to baptismal instructions a whole new perspective. Many deacon/wife couples handle these responsibilities, as well as marriage preparation in their parishes.]

CANON 907

In the celebration of the Eucharist it is not licit for deacons and lay persons to say prayers, in particular the Eucharistic prayer, or to perform actions which are proper to the celebrating priest.

While this canon is specific to the Eucharistic celebration, the concept can apply to nonliturgical functions as well. Deacons are deacons, and not priests. [See also "The Mini Priest Image," and "Something That Needs to be Said" in Chapter 9.]

CANON 910

§*1*. ***The ordinary minister of Holy Communion is a bishop, a presbyter, or a deacon.***

§2. ***The extraordinary minister of Holy Communion is an acolyte or other member of the Christian faithful deputed in accord with Canon 230*** §*3*.

This is a change from the 1917 Code that said the priest was the only minister of communion. Deacons were identified as special ministers who could only perform this ministry with the permission of their bishop or pastor, or for grave reason. Now deacons are included as ordinary Eucharistic ministers. This means that if they participate in the celebration they are required to act in this capacity. Extraordinary ministers are to be used only when there are not enough ordinary ministers of communion. [With the steady increase in the number of deacons, lay extraordinary Eucharistic ministers are being "bumped" from their "scheduled Mass." Many pastors have found it necessary to approach this potential problem with extra sensitivity.]

CANON 911

§*1*. ***The pastor or parochial vicars, chaplains and, for all who live in the house, the superior of the community in clerical religious institutes or societies of apostolic life have the right and duty to bring the Most Holy Eucharist to the sick in the form of Viaticum.***

§*2*. ***In case of necessity or with at least the presumed permission of the pastor, chaplain, or superior, who would later be notified, any priest or other minister of Holy Communion must do this.***

Viaticum, the giving of Holy Communion to a person facing the imminent danger of death, is not a normal faculty of deacons and extraordinary Eucharistic ministers. Nevertheless, they must bring Viaticum to an endangered person in the case of necessity, §2. The canon does call for proper notification thereafter. The 1972 revised Rite of Anointing, number 29, permits deacons and extraordinary ministers to give Viaticum if no priest is available, with permission.

CANON 929

In celebrating and administering the Eucharist, priests and deacons are to wear the liturgical vestments prescribed by the rubrics.

The rubrics, or official liturgical rules of the Church, referred to here are contained primarily in the General Instruction of the Roman Missal. For deacons this would mean an alb and stole of the appropriate liturgical color. The dalmatic is also an ordinary vestment for deacons, but is commonly reserved for special celebrations and processions, although this is not the formal rule. Both the dalmatic and the stole are discussed at length later in this book.

CANON 943

The minister of exposition of the Most Holy Sacrament and the Eucharistic benediction is a priest or deacon; in particular circumstances the minister of exposition and reposition only, without benediction, is an acolyte, an extraordinary minister of Holy Communion or another person deputed by the local ordinary observing prescriptions of the diocesan bishop.

Here the deacon is also identified as a normal minister during Benediction. The old 1917 Code was actually altered in 1967 to include deacons.

While the new canon allows acolytes or other deputized lay persons to expose the Holy Eucharist for adoration, they are not empowered to give the Eucharistic blessing that is central to Benediction.

CANON 1009

The orders are episcopacy, the presbyterate, and diaconate. They are conferred by the imposition of hands and by the consecratory prayer which the liturgical books prescribe for the individual grades.

This is a basic statement of who is to be considered a cleric in the Catholic Church.

CANON 1015

§*1*. ***Each candidate is to be ordained to the presbyterate or the diaconate by his own bishop or with legitimate dimissorial letters from him.***

§*2*. ***The candidate's own bishop is to ordain his own subjects personally unless he is impeded from doing so by a just cause; he cannot, however, licitly ordain a subject of an oriental rite without apostolic indult.***

§*3*. ***The person who can grant dimissorial letters to receive orders can also confer these same orders personally provided he possesses the episcopal character.***

The purpose of this canon is to set the norms for lawful ordination. First, a candidate for the priesthood or the diaconate is to be ordained by his own bishop. Another bishop can perform the ordination if the candidate's bishop provides a formal letter attesting to the candidate's worthiness and granting such permission.

This canon also reinforces the exclusiveness of bishops of the Latin Rite from those of the Oriental Rites, respecting the traditions of each as equal.

CANON 1016

As regards the diaconal ordination of those who intend to become members of the secular clergy, the proper bishop is the bishop of the diocese in which the candidate has a domicile or the diocese to which the candidate intends to devote himself; as regards the presbyteral ordination of secular clerics, the proper bishop is the bishop of the diocese into which the candidate has been incardinated through the diaconate.

While the intent of this canon is to set the rule regulating the diocese to which a priest is attached, it begins logically with the attachment established with the ordination to the diaconate. The two norms are spelled out: 1) the new deacon is attached to the bishop responsible for the area of his domicile, or to the bishop where the deacon intends to devote himself. The latter norm requires a written statement from the deacon candidate for ordination. The canonical term "incardination" indicates that attachment.

CANON 1031

§*1*. ***The presbyterate is not to be conferred upon those who have not yet completed the age of twenty-five and who do not possess sufficient maturity; an interval of at least six months is to be observed between the diaconate and the presbyterate; men destined for the presbyterate are to be admitted to the order of diaconate only after they have completed the age of twenty-three.***

§2. ***A candidate for the permanent diaconate who is not married is not to be admitted to the diaconate unless he has completed at least twenty-five years of age; if the candidate is married, he is not to be admitted to the permanent diaconate unless he has completed at least thirty-five years of age and has the consent of his wife.***

§*3*. ***The conference of bishops may determine a norm by which an older age is required for the presbyterate and the permanent diaconate.***

§*4*. ***The Apostolic See reserves to itself the dispensation from the age required in §1 and §2 when it is a question of more than one year.***

It should be noted that canon law calibrates age according to the completion of a full year of life, as marked by one's date of birth. This means that a man cannot actually be ordained a priest before the first day of his 26th year, or a permanent deacon before the first day of his 36th year.

The seond paragraph raises two considerations.

First, there is a difference between the ordination of an unmarried permanent deacon and one that is married. The concern is on the impact diaconal ministry has on a marriage. The writers of this canon wanted candidates with stable, mature marital relationships entering formation, not the recently married.

The second consideration is the canonically required consent of the wife to her husband's ordination. This is no small consideration, as is discussed earlier in this book. It is not a decision made just prior to ordination day. It is one that is first confronted during initial discernment and then repeated a couple of times during formation.

CANON 1032

§*1*. ***Candidates for the presbyterate can be promoted to the diaconate only after they have completed a five year curriculum of philosophical and theological studies.***

§*2*. ***After he has completed the curriculum of studies and before he is promoted to the presbyterate, a deacon is to participate in pastoral care, exercising his diaconal order for a suitable period of time, to be determined by the bishop or by the competent major superior.***

§*3*. ***An aspirant to the permanent diaconate is not to be promoted to that order unless he has completed the time of formation.***

After establishing the rules for formation to the priesthood, this canon applies the same concept to the permanent diaconate. Canon 236 sets out the minimal formation period of three years with allowance for the United States Conference of Bishops to spell out the guidelines for this formation.

CANON 1033

One is licitly promoted to orders only if he has received the sacrament of Confirmation.

The reception of all rites of Christian initiation has always been a requirement of orders. This canon explains why those applying for candidacy must submit proof of their baptism and confirmation when they petition for consideration.

CANON 1034

§*1.* ***An aspirant to the diaconate or the presbyterate is not to be ordained unless he has first been inscribed as a candidate by the authority mentioned in canons 1016 and 1019 in a liturgical rite of admission; this is done after he has submitted a signed petition written in his own hand and accepted in writing by the aforementioned authority.***

§*2.* ***A man who has been admitted through vows to a clerical institute is not bound to obtain this type of admission.***

Carrying on an ancient tradition, the Church still requires a candidate to formally request, in writing, that he be ordained. The bishop or appropriate authority then accepts him as a candidate in a rite of admission to candidacy. This rite replaces the abolished first tonsure, that marked the entrance into the clergy under the old Code.

CANON 1035

§*1.* ***Before anyone is promoted to either the permanent or the transitional diaconate he is required to have received the ministries of lector and acolyte and have exercised them for a suitable period of time.***

§*2.* ***Between the conferral of acolyte and diaconate, there is to be an interval of at least six months.***

While much could be written about the role of lector and acolyte as lay or installed ministries, this section will deal with it only as a logical step in the formation of a deacon. It was Pope Paul VI who drafted the basic provisions for these sequential ministries in preparation for the diaconate. They give the candidate an opportunity to adjust to liturgical ministry, the local congregation an opportunity to get used to the minister, and the Church an opportunity to evaluate the candidate. This has proven to be a very valuable process, revealing a great deal to all concerned. [The author found himself wishing he could skip the acolyte stage. It was like being a glorified altar boy. But the experience gained in liturgical functions and positive response from the parish community proved the wisdom of this step in formation.]

CANON 1036

In order to be promoted to the order of diaconate or of presbyterate the candidate is to give to his own bishop or to the competent major superior a signed declaration written in his own hand, testifying that he is about to receive sacred orders of his own accord and freely and that he will devote himself perpetually to the ecclesiastical ministry; this declaration is also to contain his petition for admission to the reception of orders.

This very self-explanatory canon derives some of its purpose from the rate of laicizations of clergy experienced by the Church during the last two decades. As a formal step, it focuses the candidate on his understanding of what he is about to do. It helps him discern his intention and commitment to a life of service.

CANON 1037

An unmarried candidate for the permanent diaconate and a candidate for the presbyterate is not to be admitted to the order of diaconate unless in a prescribed rite he has assumed publicly

before God and the Church the obligation of celibacy or professed perpetual vows in a religious institute.

This canon establishes another early part of the diaconate ordination rite. It also affirms the importance of celibacy and the candidate's commitment to it.

CANON 1039

All those who are to be promoted to some order are to make a retreat for at least five days in a place and in a manner determined by the ordinary; before he proceeds to the ordination, the bishop must be certain that the candidates have duly made this retreat.

Here the Church legislates a 5 day period of prayer and contemplation before ordination. In its wisdom, she compels the local church to set a place and time for the candidate to retreat from the world and open up to the discerned will of God. Application of this canon varies from place to place. In some areas two 3 day retreats are used for permanent deacon candidates because of the scheduling constraints caused by formation and secular occupations.

CANON 1087

Persons who are in holy orders invalidly attempt marriage.

This sparsely worded canon makes it against Church law for anyone to marry after ordination. This, applied to permanent deacons, means that if a deacon's wife dies or he has his marriage annulled, he cannot remarry. The unmarried man ordained to the permanent diaconate is subject to Canon 1087. [This one provision has caused many prospective candidates to pull back from applying. It is a sobering thought to contemplate a life alone every night after one has been happily married.]

CANON 111

§*1*. ***As long as they validly hold office, the local ordinary and the pastor can delegate to priests and deacons the faculty, even a general one, to assist at marriages within the limits of their territory.***

§*2*. ***To be valid the delegation of the faculty to assist at marriages must be given expressly to specified persons; if it is a question of special delegation, it is to be granted for a specific marriage; however, if it is a question of a general delegation, it is to be granted in writing.***

Delegation is the granting of necessary jurisdiction to witness marriages. Bishops and pastors, in their territory of authority, can grant this faculty. By this canon, deacons are given powers to witness marriages on behalf of the Church.

Several conditions are required for valid delegation of this faculty: a) a definite priest or deacon is delegated, b) the specific marriage by name of those to be married is determined, c) the delegation must be given explicitly in word or in writing, and d) the marriage must take place within the parish limits.

CANON 1169

§*1*. ***Persons who possess the episcopal character as well as presbyters to whom it is permitted by law or by legitimate concession can validly perform consecrations and dedications.***

§*2*. ***Any presbyter can impart blessings, except those which are reserved to the Roman Pontiff or to bishops.***

§*3*. ***A deacon can impart only those blessings which are expressly permitted by law.***

This canon sets out the basic norm for the giving of blessings by bishops, priests, and deacons, respectively. Each can give blessings normal to their order, and that are not specifically reserved to another hierarchical order. Most of the specific blessings are spelled out in the Roman Ritual, *De Benedictionibus* (1984).

In application, this law permits the deacon to impart a variety of blessings, but he would normally defer to a priest should one be present. Bishops and priests render blessings directly from their office as representatives of Christ. Deacons render only blessings that are invocative. That is, a deacon calls on God to impart blessing on the object of attention. They invoke or call on God through Jesus Christ to bless, rather than transmitting any type of blessing themselves.

Those blessings authorized for a deacon include:

- The blessing with the Holy Eucharist during benediction - Canon 943.
- The blessing of spouses, children, and engaged couples.
- The annual blessing of families in their home.
- The blessing of a new building, new home, and other buildings listed in the Roman Rite.
- The blessing of sick persons and elderly who are homebound.
- The blessing of associations which provide help for public needs.
- The blessing of things, places, animals, harvests, and before and after meals.
- The blessing of thanksgiving for favors received.
- The blessing of objects of devotion, including rosaries, medals, crosses, etc. - Book of Blessings, Roman Ritual - *De Benedictionibus.*

IX.

At Random

BY NOW THE READER can appreciate that the diaconate is many things to many people, and can be looked at in many ways. This section attempts to bring together several areas of concern or interest that do not fit in other parts of this book. These are reflections of and on the diaconate from unique angles.

Some of these commentaries are on the internal aspects of the diaconate, others on the externals. Some only expand on what was previously discussed, but from a different perspective. Some will seem self-evident, while others will not be understood until they are experienced. Each draws from the cumulative experience of the ever-growing community of permanent deacons in this country.

a. One, Two, And Three, In That Order

The kids have ball practice and dancing rehearsal, respectively. Your wife's car is in the shop. The boss would like to see you before you leave, and the pastor just called to have you handle a wake service for him.

The life of a permanent deacon involves more than just standing beside the priest during Mass on Sundays. It contains all the demands and obligations that anyone else would have and more. Deacons face a lifetime of dividing their time between home, work, and ministry. Those who manage this task with the least amount of disruption to all concerned are those who have learned to put things in perspective, to set priorities.

It is very easy to place too much emphasis on one facet of life. Workaholics make this an art form. They live to work, rather than working to live. Those in ministry, especially those new to ministry, often exhibit the same type of imbalance in their lives. They live to do one ministerial thing after another. They are driven to do more "for God," at the expense of all the other relationships and obligations they have. It is unthinkable for them to say "no" when it is something for the Church.

This situation makes as much sense as a newly married man failing to show up for work because he cannot leave his bride's side. It makes as much sense as either parent ignoring their spouse to give all their time and attention to their children. In other words, it doesn't make sense when it is looked at logically. The problem is, it is not looked at logically.

The logic that God gave the deacon a wife before children, and the skills to maintain a livelihood to sustain them is ignored. The logic behind him being Christ in the work place is disregarded in exchange for doing ministry. This situation is not always a major problem, nor is it without justification in the mind of the deacon involved. It is normally only enough of a problem to be irritating to the others affected, and easily explained by the one causing it.

The ones negatively affected the most are the family. Weekends, that used to be time together, become filled with "church stuff." More and more weeknights are taken up with meetings, wakes, or counseling. Even when the family goes out, dad always seems to be talking to someone about their problems, or he talks to his family like he was doing a Sunday sermon.

Employers can also become irritated with this situation. They have hired an employee, not a company chaplain.

The answer to this situation lies in the setting of clearcut priorities within one's life. These priorities determine which facet of life will get preference when time and attention decisions have to be made. Once the first has been taken care of, then the second can be responded to, etc. These priorities should be:

***One** - Family,* ***Two** - Job,* ***Three** - Diaconate.*

The other ordained orders in the Church, bishops and priests, have as their job their ministry. Also they have no family waiting for them to come home to supper. In most cases, they don't have to commute to work, play the career advancement game, or cut the grass and paint the trim on the house over the weekend. They definitely don't have to take their kids to dancing class and baseball practice three times a week, or visit their in-laws.

The permanent deacon adds his ministry to the other aspects of his life. He brings his ministry into his workplace. He, in the majority of cases, is living in another sacrament that was prior to Holy Orders. His responsibilities, be they financial, physical, or emotional dictate how he must prioritize his decisions. He must give himself permission to say "no" to the ever-increasing demands others will place on him, if he lets them. He must be ready to minister to himself by giving himself some of his valuable time and attention. Deacons need to live a balanced life in Christ.

b. Don't Forget Your Visibility

"Priests are people too!" is a catchy phrase that confronts the tendency of many inside and outside of the Church to hold our clergy to a higher standard of conduct than the rest of society. But remember, deacons are clergy also.

A newly ordained deacon said to the Director of the diocesan diaconate formation program: "You know, you never prepared us for driving in rush hour traffic, and waiting in the checkout line at the supermarket.'' The puzzled Director was then given the following account of what the new deacon had recently experienced.

''The other day when driving home from work I was stuck in some pretty bad traffic. It was like everybody on the road was determined to cut me off, or slow me down. Just about the time I was about to blow my top, this guy in the next lane absentmindedly cuts me off. Then he crawls along at five miles slower than the speed limit. When I got my chance, I swung into the next lane and was going to pull up beside him and give him a piece of my mind.

''Do you know what he did? He waved and smiled. I could read his lips as he said, 'congratulations!' Boy was I blown away.

''Still getting over that incident, I stopped off at the grocery to pick up milk and bread. I went to the express line but was behind four people, each with more than the maximum ten items. I stood there and stood there. Three of them paid with checks, requiring the manager's approval. By the time I made it to the register I wanted to chew somebody out, anybody. I didn't care who. That's when the checkout girl, whom I've never met before in my life, says, 'Oh, Deacon! I was at your first Mass, Sunday, and I really enjoyed your sermon. You were really talking to me, and where I'm at in my life. Thank you.' ''

Yes, a lay person can do everything a deacon can, under the right circumstances. But when they are not doing these ministries they are judged just like any other person in the pew. Deacons are not.

Assisting during the Eucharist, and preaching may make up only a small part of a deacon's ministry, but it is the most visible part. In one hour he can make contact with literally hundreds of people. More people and faces than he could ever remember the next time he is in a shopping center or at a ball game. They on the other hand, will recognize his face wherever he is, and maybe more importantly, whatever he is doing.

The man ordained to the permanent diaconate loses much of his private life. He becomes a public figure. What he does, or doesn't do, is now judged differently than before. This means that things he did before will be reacted to while they would have been ignored in the past. Minor mistakes in judgment, or even the simple act of buying the Swimsuit issue of *Sports Illustrated* will be criticized, all because he is a deacon. This may not be fair, just, or even Christian, but it will happen. Also, it will happen to a deacon's immediate family members.

This is not something to think about only by the man interested in responding to this calling. It is something to be remembered by all present deacons.

c. The "Mini Priest" Image

There is no image more rejected by the diaconal community than that of the "mini priest." This derogatory term is used by those questioning the need for the permanent diaconate. It effectively points out, with a stabbing finger, all that deacons should not be.

The level of this concern is dramatically recorded in the May, 1986 issue of *U.S. Catholic*. Each month this publication sends out copies of articles they plan to publish, along with several related questions. A representative sample of their subscribers are polled, and their responses are printed with the article. The article in question was "Permanent deacons shouldn't play priest," by Msgr. Ernest J. Fielder.

Some of the questions, and the answers given are very revealing.

Question - "When I see a permanent deacon wearing a Roman collar, I think he's trying to look like a priest."

55% agree   22% disagree   23% other

Question - "Despite theology to the contrary, the image of permanent deacons in my parish is that he is a servant of the priest."

36% agree	40% disagree	24% other

Question - "A deacon is as much an ordained minister as a priest and therefore should be able to wear a Roman collar if he chooses."

20% agree	72% disagree	8% other

Question - "Along with Msgr. Fielder, I think permanent deacons shouldn't try to look and act like priests."

82% agree	9% disagree	9% other

Msgr. Fielder wrote:

"Should permanent deacons participate at Mass? No. And yes. Is this a cop-out answer? Not really; in fact, a clue to my preference is found in the word order of my response. No is my first answer because Catholics do not need another official performer at Mass — especially if lay people in the church can do all or most of the same things. No, if the liturgical ministry of the deacon is seen as his only identifying characteristic. No, if this is his most prominent ministry."

Doing those things that a priest does, or even looking like one, generates a great deal of concern and criticism from many areas of the Church. The accomplishments of the post-Vatican II Church seem somehow threatened by over-clericalism and over-ritualization. The role of lay persons is seen as particularly threatened. While these are only perceived problems in some communities, they are real in others.

The answer, like so many questions pertaining to the diaconate, is not simple. It lies not only with the selection-formation process for deacons, or the diocesan implementation of these programs, but with the understanding of ordained ministry.

Individuals attracted to the diaconate only by the pretty white albs, colorful stoles, and pageantry of the liturgy must be rejected. A deacon may be described as a server within the local church, but that doesn't translate into altar server, or "super altar boy." The diaconate cannot be looked on as some type of reward for "good-ole boys" who have spent years in volunteer work in the parish.

The emphasis placed on true *diakonia*, service, must come from the diocese itself. The local church must lead its community of deacons towards specific goals, and away from those things that confuse the diaconate with the priesthood. This begins in the formation program, and should continue past ordination with ongoing evaluations.

A number of dioceses have responded to the most visible sign of this problem. They direct their deacons not to wear the Roman collar, except in very unique situations. Regulations on the liturgical role of deacons, appropriate rubrics, and even liturgical garb have been reviewed in recent years to address the related issues.

Many criticisms have been eliminated simply through diocesan-wide educational programs on the diaconate. It is still a fact of life that there are dioceses that do not have diaconate programs. Even in dioceses with such programs, ignorance about the diaconate can still be widespread. Instruction in what the diaconate should be makes for a congregation that will accept nothing less.

Of course, this instruction should include an explanation of all ordained ministries, since it is by comparison that understanding comes — understanding of the priesthood and the diaconate.

Here an observation is offered on the perceived role of the parish priest in this country.

Ask the average Catholic parishioner what their priest does and you will hear a list of sacramental and liturgical duties. Ask them what he does all day and you will probably get a vague answer indicating a few random activities and a lot of free time to do as he wishes. The perception of today's priest by the majority of Catholics is sadly lacking.

It is only after extensive direct contact with a parish priest's life that his lifestyle, his role in the community, and his ministry are understood. If one didn't think about it much, one would never realize that priests never have weekends off, like lay people. Priests more often than not have to get up fairly early to "begin work," presiding at Mass. They are constantly on call for counseling, confessions, problem solving, visits to the sick and dying, and for comfort to the bereaved. Active lay people attend one or two parish meetings a month. The pastor attends most of them for all the organizations in the parish, and these normally are at night, after his full day "at work."

The liturgical role of the priest, with the pretty vestments and ceremony, is only part of his priestly ministry. It is the most visible, to the most people, but it is only a small part of what he does.

This observation is made to shed light on what the full ministry of a permanent deacon should be; only part of it is liturgical. None of it should be a replacement of priestly ministry. As a matter of fact, the Revised Code of Canon Law, 1983, spells out this prohibition pertaining to liturgical matters. Canon 907 prohibits deacons from performing liturgical actions proper to priests, such as reciting the Eucharistic prayer.

d. Is Permanent A Permanent Title?

If there are only about 250 transitional deacons in the ministry in this country at any given time, isn't it odd that they are addressed as "deacon" while the 9,400 others of this same hierarchical rank are called "permanent deacon"?

Admittedly there was a need to distinguish between these two types of deacons during the restoration period of the diaconate.

"Married deacon" seems to be the term most used in Church documents and even in the revised 1983 Code of Canon Law as a result of the groundwork of the Second Vatican Council. The mindset of 800 years was nothing to be ignored.

The question on the horizon now is of the continued need for the prefix. As one very knowledgeable observer commented, "It's like the tail wagging the dog. 'Permanent deacon' places emphasis in the wrong place." *Diakonia*, service, is the focal point, not a permanent status.

This may be a non-issue in some circles, but it speaks directly to the identity of diaconate. It is suggested that in the future, dropping of the "permanent" prefix would further a clearer understanding of the order. Transitional deacons could be then rightly addressed so as to acknowledge their rank and temporary status. Deacons, the ordinary kind not the temporary kind, will emerge as an integral part of the whole that is the Church, the Body of Christ.

e. Deacons Didn't Steal The Stole

A 1988 issue of the *Liguorian* magazine featured an article entitled, "Who is that guy with the side-ways stole?" It was a very thorough piece on the restored permanent diaconate. The cover of the magazine featured a picture of a deacon wearing an alb and the indicated stole. This is a prime example of how this liturgical vestment, so worn, has become the symbol of the diaconate to many Christians.

A closer look at this general perception reveals that many see the deacon's use of the stole only as a means to indicate that one is a cleric, but not a priest. This impression is encouraged by the "traditional" deacon stole that is a straight strip of fabric, like the priest's stole, in comparison to the "contemporary" deacon stole that is cut to hang smoothly across the torso, then straight down along the right side.

But is the deacon stole really just something taken from the presbyterate?

The 1908 edition of *The Catholic Encyclopedia* indicated that it is not. "We possess few references to the stole anterior to the 9th century. In the East, however, it is mentioned very early, the deacon's stole being frequently referred to even in the 4th and 5th centuries. The priest's stole is not mentioned in the East until the 8th century. The stole is first mentioned in the West in the 6th and 7th centuries."

This article of clothing can be traced back to pre-New Testament times. It was worn by Roman authorities in many Greek-speaking cities and states, to indicate a particular rank or office. Its origin also is related to the liturgical napkin, which deacons are said to have carried (referring back to the table waiting job description of the first 7 deacons, one would imagine).

Both the 1908 *Catholic Encyclopedia* and 9th century Church artwork and manuscript illustrations indicate deacons wore the stole straight down from their left shoulder, especially in the West. Certainly, it was natural for them to begin wearing the stole across the body, as time passed, if for no other reason than to keep it from falling off the shoulder. (We are talking about the pre-velcro Middle Ages.)

The history of the stole, its use in different ages and different areas of the world is interesting. The one thing it reveals is that deacons didn't steal the stole from priests, but rather that it was accepted as a correct indicator of office as originally used by deacons.

This being the case, maybe future deacon stoles could be cut and ornamented for the way they are worn. Instead of having things on the diagonal as if a priest's stole was being modified, place symbols vertical to the floor. It's a thought.

f. What The Fully Vested Deacon Wears

In the contemporary Church the liturgical vestments for permanent deacons, as we have seen, seem to consist only of an alb and the diagonally worn stole. Yet there is another vestment peculiar to this order. It is the dalmatic.

Modeled after the ancient Roman square-cut tunic, it is formally described as: "An outer liturgical vestment with short open sleeves, and opening for the head, and open at the sides from the hem to the shoulders. It reaches to or below the knee and is worn by the deacon at solemn Mass or processions. It is so named because originally it was made from Dalmatian wool. This garment has become an auxiliary, or optional vestment worn by the deacon as assistant at a pontifical function." (*The Catholic Encyclopedia*, 1967)

The history of this vestment is not perfectly clear. As with many externals in the early Church, it was adopted in some areas and not in others, or used in different ways in different local churches. Joseph Dahmus' *Dictionary of Medieval Civilization* reports: "In early centuries it was worn by bishops, and from the fourth century by deacons as well." *The New Catholic Encyclopedia* says: "It was first used by the Roman noble class. A square cut tunic, it normally featured two 'clavi,' vertical stripes, down the front and back, either in red or purple. Common opinion indicates that the popes used it first, and by the 4th century they awarded it to Roman deacons. By the 12th century it was the vestment for all deacons."

The 1908 *Catholic Encyclopedia* gives a little more detail into the question:

"The dalmatic itself, which is not regarded as distinctive of the deacon, was originally confined to the deacons of Rome, and to wear such a vestment outside of Rome was conceded by the early popes as a special privilege.

"On the other hand, it is practically certain that dalmatics were worn in Rome both by the pope and by his deacons in the latter half of the fourth century. As to the manner of wearing, after the 10th century it was only in Milan and Southern Italy that deacons carried the stole over the dalmatic, but at an earlier date, this had been common in many parts of the West.''

The one thing that seems certain is the difference between the priestly chasuble and the dalmatic. The chasuble is a sleeveless round cut outermost vestment, worn since the 9th century by the presider at Mass, either the bishop or priest. Interestingly, Rev. H.J. McCloud's *Clerical Dress and Insignia of the Roman Catholic Church* indicates that the popes since the 8th century wore both, and other bishops since about the 10th century.

(New episcopal rubrics promulgated at the end of 1989 return to this practice.)

As to the proper use of the dalmatic today, Father Kenneth Hedrick, Director of the Office of Worship, Archdiocese of New Orleans, says the dalmatic may be worn whenever a priest would wear the chasuble. ''The common practice is that it is saved for special occasions, and major feasts.'' says Fr. Hedrick. ''In the Roman Rite the dalmatic is the outermost vestment. So the stole is worn under it. I think the recent practice of wearing the stole over it was reinvented by church supply firms.''

Fr. Hedrick has expressed concern about the custom-made dalmatics that ignore basic considerations for vesture. He says there should be a unity of vesture, at the very least a sameness, on the altar. He cites the visual impact of a lime green dalmatic next to a kelly green chasuble during Mass. Only the totally color blind would not appreciate this concern.

An interesting footnote: The dalmatic's name refers to the fine wool produced in ancient Dalmatia, the present day Yugoslavian coastal area on the Adriatic Sea. One of the towns of this region is the sheep herding community of Medjugorje.

g. A Life Of Service

It is so very easy to say, "A life of service." It has a nice ring to it. It is such a positive, approvable idea. How can one go wrong with it?

Well, one way is to ignore just how long a life can be. Then one could forget the basic element of life, change.

To project a life in the diaconate based on repeating the same liturgical actions weekly, or on the three year cycle of homilies based on the Gospels is rather limited, to say the least. Planning to minister to God's people comfortably in one's own parish may be a miserly use of one's gifts and graces. Failing to take into consideration change in ministry, or in the lives of one's neighbors, can only lead to little that is worth the effort to get there.

A life of service in an ordained ministry must be marked by a selflessness that empowers, not limits. It must be truly open to the unforeseen will of God.

Take for example the newly ordained permanent deacon, with his loving wife beside him. She has been with him through it all. It is she, as an enabling gift from God, who helped him to become what he is. She helped him respond to the Father's call. What would his life of service become if the Father called that gift, his wife, home to Him? Would he still be an effective minister of service if he was not open to the will and healing graces available to him through the Son of God?

Not all changes in life are that soul-shaking, but they do have their impact. Take for example the transfer of a pastor who understands and uses deacons for one who does not. Or the reassignment of a deacon from parish work to a ministry with the sick or the poor.

What happens to a life of service when a man loses his secular job? Or what happens when he is offered a major promotion, but with a transfer to another state or area that has not implemented a diaconate program? Does one let his ministry affect his decision about applying for a particular job? Does one let his ministry affect his decision about where he would buy that new house the family has always wanted?

Like so many of the ideas raised in this section, there is no one set of answers. Each individual must come to terms with his own life of service, and through prayer and openness to the will of God, find the right answer for them.

h. Something That Needs To Be Said

Rather than dancing around the issue, let's get it right out in the open. Let's put it in print for all to read.

SOME PRIESTS JUST CAN'T STAND DEACONS!

There it is. It is an undeniable fact of life. For a variety of reasons, there are still some priests who would rather go through life not having to deal with permanent deacons in any fashion. They just don't have any use for them.

Why? That's hard to say. Many in this category are silent about their dislikes. The ones who do speak out do so from behind a collection of individual incidents, some from the early days of restoration, others without too many specifics.

Speak to more than three permanent deacons at a gathering and you will probably hear an example of this attitude. The situation is better today than it was for the first permanent deacons ordained, but the problem still exists. New deacons, and those preparing for this ministry, should be advised of this situation.

It can manifest itself in many ways. Some pastors will not let permanent deacons do any independent ministry or liturgical functions within their parish. Others will not let deacons preach or witness marriages in their church. Periodically a permanent deacon will report that a certain priest will not do anything where a deacon's wife is involved. Other deacons are neutralized at all levels of their planned ministry by the behind-the-scene conduct of the local priest.

Not all of this is caused by strict conservative or overly traditional attitudes. Some instances of this situation are caused by really bad experiences with truly incompetent permanent deacons. Others are caused by a poor theological understanding of this office. Still other negative reactions to the diaconate are caused by the insecurities of certain priests: the proximity of women, i.e. deacon's wives, and perceived threats to their position or power.

Before going any farther, it must be pointed out that these comments refer to the minority, not the majority. The permanent diaconate could not have thrived as it has if this were not so. Most priests do enjoy having deacons around. They do support and understand their role and ministry. Even priests who were once openly cautious when the order was first restored are now some of its strongest advocates. They, like others, admit to the greater sensitivity they have gained while ministering with deacon/wife couples.

The obstinate minority, though, stick out like a sore thumb. They can make the most dedicated deacon question the worth of his efforts. Priests who can't stand permanent deacons messing around in their territory can be very damaging to their local faith community.

The Church's vast experience of priest/deacon relationships proves this type of situation is not necessary. Unfortunately or fortunately, the means to resolving this problem lies within the diaconal community.

Permanent deacons, clerics with wives, are the new kids on the block. They are still a novelty. The congregation reacts to them in a more visible fashion than to their priests. Deacons can be the key to solving this situation, or they can become self-righteous and only foster it in others. It is up to them to go out of their way to minimize their pastor's fears or bruised ego. It is up to the deacons to minister to priests, as they would to the laity. It is up to deacons to be as correct as they can be, to eliminate reasons for general criticism of all permanent deacons.

No one will be liked by everyone. Nor will deacons be accepted by everyone. Still it is the clerics' role to be Christ-like in all things, and a stumbling block to none. As to those in the presbyterate who cannot handle this new stressor in their lives, pray for them out of the love Jesus calls each to have for his brother.

i. Why

In as much as this book attempts to deal with the general question, "Are you called to a life of service?" one last specific question has to be asked. ***Why?*** Why become a permanent deacon?

This simple but penetrating question is the focal point of the discernment process. It is also a means by which others can come to terms with this order, whether they be family, clergy, religious, or laity. Archdiocese of New Orleans Diaconate Director, Dean Jim Swiler says this is a bottom-line question:

"We make sure the proposed applicants to the program understand that there is really nothing a permanent deacon can do that a lay person in the modern Church cannot do. This is sometimes a very sobering thought."

Under special circumstances, any approved lay person can witness a sacramental marriage, or give a homily-like reflection during the liturgy. Lay people everywhere are installed as extraordinary Eucharistic Ministers, bring the Eucharist to the sick, and conduct prayer services. They also, as any baptized person can, baptize as the need dictates. This is equally true for women as it is for men.

So why the need for three or more years of training? Why a life-long commitment to obedience to the bishop, and a modified vow of celibacy? Why?

For those called by name, even from the darkness of their mother's womb, the "why question" should be most powerful. When answered openly and honestly, it will reveal the true meaning of diaconate. No further definition or explanation will be necessary for that man. His answer says it all.

There are answers to this question, but not "the answer." Each person has to come to terms with how he will respond, or if there is a reason to respond.

Whatever the individual decision, the true differences between the diaconate and lay ministry still stand. They stem from the collegiality of the order, and more importantly, the sacramental power of grace.

To continue a lifetime of service there must be more than good intentions. There also must be commitment, true, but if support is lacking, all the determination and commitment in the world will not sustain it. One of the identifying characteristics of the permanent diaconate is community. Deacons support deacons. They each experience or suffer exactly what the others have. They each know what impact this calling has on their family, their lifestyle, and even their emotional health. They know the exhilaration and satisfaction resulting from helping others just by being there. They know the feelings of helplessness in the face of tragedy.

This is not to imply that the other members of the clergy do not support each other, or do not support deacons. It's just that their situations and backgrounds are different. Sometimes it takes someone who has had an argument with his wife, or a fight with his teenager, or a cut in pay or benefits from his employer to help someone else in ministry who is going through these problems. When the unique dynamics of ordained ministry are added to these circumstances the need is all the more acute. Diaconal communities strive to meet this need in a compassionate and prayerful manner.

More intrinsic to the diaconate is the sacramental grace that empowers it. It is this facet of the ministry that is all too often overlooked in discussions of it. Where there is unbalanced attention paid to the functional or operational aspects of the diaconate the difference between it and lay ministry are blurred or erased. But it is this sacramental difference that makes it what it truly is.

Consider for a moment what the Church teaches about the priesthood and the Mystical Body of Christ, the faithful, in the Decree on the Ministry and Life of Priests, *Presbyterorum Ordinis*, par. 2:

> . . . for in that Body all the faithful are made a holy and kingly priesthood, they offer spiritual sacrifices to God through Jesus Christ, and they proclaim the virtues of him who has called them out of darkness into his admirable light.

We are all part of that priesthood, each member of the Church. This does not mean that there is no need for ordained priests, though. The above document goes on to say:

> However, the Lord also appointed certain men as ministers, in order that they might be united in one body in which "all the members have not the same function." (Romans 12:4)

So too, the diaconate is called to perform functions similar to both the laity and the priesthood. This is clearly the intent of the Second Vatican Council, in *Lumen Gentium*, the Dogmatic Constitution on the Church, par. 29:

> At a lower level of the hierarchy are to be found deacons, who receive the imposition of hands "not unto the priesthood, but unto the ministry." For, strengthened by sacramental grace they are dedicated to the People of God, in conjunction with the bishop and his body of priests, in service of the liturgy, of the Gospel, and of works of charity.

So, why the diaconate? Because it is a calling, a special calling from the Lord. Just as He called twelve men to be His apostles, He calls certain men today to fulfill the roles His Church has established through the guidance of the Holy Spirit. The diaconate is a calling, a vocation — not a right, not a reward, not a thing one does because it is a good thing to do.

If a man discerns that he is not called to this ministry, the very fact that he drew closer to Jesus to find this out is a wondrous thing. Many are called, and it is true that few are chosen. The calling to discernment may be like that of St. Matthias, something eventual. Then again, it may be an opportunity for yet unrevealed graces.

The thing to remember is the Will of God, not the will of man. How and why God does what He does, is beyond our feeble intellects. We can come to understand it only as He permits, not through the application of logic or what man calls justice. The diaconate is not a right, it is a gift. It can be accepted because it is offered. Why it is offered remains to be revealed, in His time.

X.

Epilogue

THE AUTHOR could not think of any better way to conclude this work than by providing the reader with the text of Pope John Paul II's historic talk to the American diaconal community and their wives. This was given during his September 19, 1987, visit to Detroit, Michigan. Approximately 2,000 couples, representing deacons from across the United States, gathered to hear His Holiness. Those present reported such a strong feeling of warmth and anticipation that they could almost see it. Their patience was well rewarded.

To give any type of commentary or analysis of this talk would be presumptuous. Yet the Holy Father made numerous points that deserve, if not demand, close attention. The reader is invited to listen to the Pope's message as they read his words. He speaks on many levels, in a deceptively simple style. His talk is truly a complete summation of this entire book, or for that matter any work on the diaconate. For example, his opening greeting validates and elevates all of this order, and their wives.

The text is printed here as it was on the copies issued to the media on the day of the gathering.

Dear Brothers in the Service of Our Lord.

Dear Wives and Collaborators of these men ordained to the Permanent Diaconate.

I greet you in the love of our Lord Jesus Christ, in whom, as Saint Paul tells us, God has chosen us, redeemed us and adopted us as his children (cf. Eph 1:3 ff.). Together with Saint Paul, and together with you today, I praise our heavenly Father for these wonderful gifts of grace.

It is a special joy for me to meet with you because you represent a great and visible sign of the working of the Holy Spirit in the wake of the Second Vatican Council, which provided for the restoration of the permanent diaconate in the Church. The wisdom of that provision is evident in your presence in such numbers today and in the fruitfulness of your ministries. With the whole Church, I give thanks to God for the call you have received and for your generous response. For the majority of you who are married, this response has been made possible by the love and support and collaboration of your wives. It is a great encouragement to know that in the United States over the past two decades almost eight thousand permanent deacons have been ordained for the service of the Gospel.

It is above all the call to service that I wish to celebrate with you today. In speaking of deacons, the Vatican Council said that "strengthened by sacramental grace, in communion with the Bishop and his presbyterate, they serve the People of God in the service of the liturgy, the word, and charity" (*Lumen Gentium*, 29). Reflecting further on this description, my predecessor Paul VI was in agreement with the Council that "the permanent diaconate should be restored as a driving force for the Church's service (*diakonia*) toward the local Christian communities, and as a sign or sacrament of the Lord Christ himself, who 'came not to be served but to serve' " (*Ad Pascendum*), August 15, 1972, Introduction). These words recall the ancient tradition of the Church as expressed by the early Fathers such as Ignatius of Antioch, who says that deacons are "ministers of the mysteries of Jesus Christ . . . ministers of the Church of God" (*Ad Trallianos*, II, 3). You, dear brothers, belong to the life of the Church that goes back to saintly deacons, like Lawrence, and before him to Stephen and his companions, who the Acts of the Apostles consider "deeply spiritual and prudent" (Acts 6:3).

This is at the very heart of the diaconate to which you have been called: to be a servant of the mysteries of Christ and, at one and the same time, to be servant of your brothers and sisters. That these two dimensions are inseparably joined together in one reality shows the important nature of the ministry which is yours by ordination.

How are we to understand the mysteries of Christ of which you are ministers? A profound description is given to us by Saint Paul in the reading we heard a few moments ago. The central mystery is this: God the Father's plan of glory to bring all things in the heavens and on earth into one under the headship of Christ, his beloved Son. It is for this that all the baptized are predestined, chosen, redeemed and sealed with the Holy Spirit. This plan of God is at the center of our lives and the life of the world.

At the same time, if service to this redemptive plan is the mission of all the baptized, what is the specific dimension of your service as deacons? The Second Vatican Council explains that a sacramental grace conferred through the imposition of hands enables you to carry out your service of the word, the altar and charity with a special effectiveness (cf. *Ad Gentes*, 16). The service of the deacon is the Church's service sacramentalized. Yours is not just one ministry among others, but it is truly meant to be, as Paul VI described it, a "driving force" for the Church's *diakonia*. By your ordination you are configured to Christ in his servant role. You are also meant to be living signs of the servanthood of his Church.

If we keep in mind the deep spiritual nature of this *diakonia*, then we can better appreciate the interrelation of the three areas of ministry traditionally associated with the diaconate, that is, the ministry of the word, the ministry of the altar, and the ministry of charity. Depending on the circumstances, one or another of these may receive particular emphasis in an individual deacon's work, but these three ministries are inseparably joined together as one in the service of God's redemptive plan. This is so because the word of God inevitably leads us to the Eucharistic worship of God at the altar; in turn, this worship leads us to a new way of living which expresses itself in acts of charity.

This charity is both love of God and love of neighbor. As the First Letter of John teaches us, "One who has no love for the brother he has seen cannot love the God he has not seen . . . whoever loves God must also love his brothers" (1 Jn 4:20-21). By the same token, acts of charity which are not rooted in the word of God and in worship cannot bear lasting fruit. "Apart from me," Jesus says, "you can do nothing" (Jn 15:5). The ministry of charity is confirmed on every page of the Gospel; it demands a constant and radical conversion of heart. We have a forceful example of this in the Gospel of Matthew, proclaimed earlier. We are told: "offer no resistance to injury." We are commanded: "love your enemies and pray for your persecutors." All of this is an essential part of the ministry of charity.

Certainly today's world is not lacking opportunities for such a ministry, whether in the form of the simplest acts of charity or the most heroic witness to the radical demands of the Gospel. All around us many of our brothers and sisters live in either spiritual or material poverty or both. So many of the world's people are oppressed by injustice and the denial of their fundamental human rights. Still others are troubled or suffer from a loss of faith in God, or are tempted to give up hope.

In the midst of the human condition it is a great source of satisfaction to learn that so many permanent deacons in the United States are involved in direct service to the needy; to the ill, the abused and battered, the young and old, the dying and bereaved, the deaf, blind and disabled, those who have known suffering in their marriages, the homeless, victims of substance abuse, prisoners, refugees, street people, the rural poor, the victims of racial and ethnic discrimination, and many others. As Christ tells us, "as often as you did it for one of my least brothers, you did it for me." (Mt 25:40).

At the same time, the Second Vatican Council reminds us that the ministry of charity at the service of God's redemptive plan also obliges us to be a positive influence for change in the world in which we live, that is, to be leaven — to be the soul of human society — so that society may be renewed by Christ and transformed into the family of God (cf. *Gaudium et Spes*, 40 ff.). The "temporal order includes marriage and the family, the world of culture, economic and social life, the trades and professions, political institutions, the solidarity of peoples, and issues of justice and peace" (cf. *Apostolicam Actuositatem* 7; *Gaudium et Spes*, 46 ff.). The task is seldom an easy one. The truth about ourselves and the world, revealed in the Gospel is not always what the world wants to hear. Gospel truth often contradicts commonly accepted thinking, as we see so clearly today with regards to evils such as racism, contraception, abortion, and euthanasia — to name just a few.

Taking an active part in society belongs to the baptismal mission of every Christian in accordance with his or her state in life, but the permanent deacon has a special witness to give. The sacramental grace of his ordination is meant to strengthen him and to make his efforts fruitful, even as his secular occupation gives him entry into the temporal sphere in a way that is normally not appropriate for other members of the clergy. At the same time, the fact that he is an ordained minister of the Church brings a special dimension to his efforts in the eyes of those with whom he lives and works.

Equally important is the contribution that a married deacon makes to the transformation of family life. He and his wife, having entered into a communion of life, are called to help and serve each other (cf. *Gaudium et Spes*, 48). So intimate is their partnership and unity in the sacrament of marriage, that the Church fittingly requires the wife's consent before her husband can be ordained a permanent deacon (Can. 1031 §2). As the current guidelines for the permanent diaconate in the United States point out, the nurturing and deepening of mutual, sacrificial love between husband and wife constitute perhaps the most significant involvement of a deacon's wife in her husband's public ministry in the Church (*Guidelines*, NCCB, p. 110). Today especially, this is no small service.

In particular, the deacon and his wife must be a living example of fidelity and indissolubility in Christian marriage before a world which is in dire need of such signs. By facing in a spirit of faith the challenges of married life and the demands of daily living, they strengthen the family life not only of the Church community but of the whole of society. They also show how the obligations of family, work and ministry can be harmonized in the service of the Church's mission. Deacons and their wives and children can be a great encouragement to all others who are working to promote family life.

Mention must also be made of another kind of family, namely the parish, which is the usual setting in which the vast majority of deacons fulfill the mandate of their ordination "to help the Bishop and his presbyterate." The parish provides an ecclesial context for your ministry and services as a reminder that your labors are not carried out in isolation, but in communion with the Bishop, his priest and all those who in varying degrees share in the public ministry of the Church. Permanent deacons have an obligation to respect the office of the priest and to cooperate conscientiously and generously with him and with the parish staff. The deacon also has a right to be accepted and fully recognized by them and by all for what he is: an ordained minister of the word, the altar and charity.

Given the dignity and importance of the permanent diaconate, what is expected of you? As Christians we must not be ashamed to speak of the qualities of a servant to which all believers must aspire, and especially deacons, whose ordination rite describes them as "servants of all." A deacon must be known for fidelity, integrity and obedience, and so it is that fidelity to Christ, moral integrity and obedience to the Bishop must mark your lives, as the ordination rite makes clear (cf. also *Ad Pascendum*, Introduction). In that rite the Church also expresses her hopes and expectations for you when she prays:

> "Lord, may they excel in every virtue; in love . . . concern . . . unassuming authority . . . self discipline and in holiness of life. May their conduct exemplify your commandments and lead your people to imitate their purity of life. May they remain strong and steadfast in Christ, giving to the world the witness of a pure conscience. May they . . . imitate your Son, who came, not to be served but to serve."

Dear brothers: this prayer commits you to lifelong spiritual formation so that you may grow and persevere in rendering a service that is truly edifying to the People of God. You who are wives of permanent deacons, being close collaborators in their ministry, are likewise challenged with them to grow in the knowledge and love of Jesus Christ. And this of course means growth in prayer — personal prayer, family prayer, liturgical prayer.

Since deacons are ministers of the word, the Second Vatican Council invites you to constant reading and diligent study of the Sacred Scriptures, lest — if you are a preacher — you become an empty one for failing to hear the word in your own heart (cf. *Dei Verbum*, 25). In your lives as deacons you are called to hear and guard and do the word of God, in order to be able to proclaim it worthily. To preach to God's people is an honor that entails a serious preparation and real commitment to holiness of life.

As ministers of the altar you must be steeped in the spirit of the liturgy, and be convinced above all that it is "the summit toward which the activity of the Church is directed and at the same time the source from which all her power flows" (cf. *Sacrosanctum Concilium*, 10). You are called to discharge your office with the dignity and reverence befitting the liturgy, which the Council powerfully describes as being "above all the worship of the divine majesty" (ibid., 33). I join you in thanking all those who devote themselves to your training, both before and after your ordination, through programs of spiritual, theological, and liturgical formation.

"Sing a new song unto the Lord! Let your song be sung from mountains high!" Sing to him as servants, but also sing as friends of Christ, who has made known to you all that he has heard from the Father. It was not you who chose him, but he who chose you, to go forth and bear fruit — fruit that will last. This you do loving one another (cf. Jn 15:15 ff.). By the standards of this world, servanthood is despised, but in the wisdom and providence of God it is the mystery through which Christ redeems the world. And you are ministers of that mystery, heralds of that Gospel. You can be sure that one day you will hear the Lord saying to each of you: "Well done, good and faithful servant, enter into the joy of your Lord." (cf. Mt 25:21).

Dear brothers and sisters: as one who strives to be "the servant of the servants of the Lord," I cannot take leave of you until, together, we turn to Mary, as she continues to proclaim: "I am the servant of the Lord" (Lk 1:38). And in the example of her servanthood we see the perfect model of our own call to the discipleship of our Lord Jesus Christ and to the service of his Church.

Bibliography

Achtemeier, Paul J., *Harper's Bible Dictionary*, San Francisco, CA: Harper and Row, 1985.

Broderick, Robert C., *The Catholic Encyclopedia*, New York, NY: Thomas Nelson Publishing, 1976.

Chapin, John, *The Book of Catholic Quotations*, New York, NY: Farar, Straus and Cudahy, 1956.

Code, Community, Ministry, Washington, D.C.: Canon Law Society of America, 1983.

Code of Canon Law, Latin-English Edition, Washington, D.C.: Canon Law Society of America, 1983.

Code of Canon Law: A Text and Commentary, Washington, D.C.: Canon Law Society of America, 1984.

Dahmus, Joseph, *Dictionary of Medieval Civilization*, New York, NY: Macmillan Publishing Co., 1984.

''Deacon'', *Encyclopedia Britannica*, New York, NY: 1910.

''Deacons'', *The Catholic Encyclopedia*, New York, NY: Robert Appleton Company, 1908.

''Deacon'', *The New Catholic Encyclopedia*, New York, NY: McGraw Hill, 1967.

''Deacon'', *The New Schaff-Herzog Encyclopedia of Religious Knowledge*, Grand Rapids, MI: Baker Book House, 1950.

Delaney, John J., *Dictionary of Saints*, Garden City, NY: Doubleday and Company, 1980.

Huels, John M., OSM, JCD, *The Pastoral Companion: A Canon Law Handbook for Catholic Ministry*, Chicago, IL: Franciscan Herald Press, 1986.

Kwatera, Michael, OSB, *The Liturgical Ministry of Deacons*, Collegeville, MN: Liturgical Press, 1985.

McBrien, Richard P., *Catholicism*, Minneapolis, MN: Winston Press, 1981.

McCaslin, Patrick and Michael G. Lawler, *Sacrament of Service*, New York, NY: Paulist Press, 1986.

McCloud, Rev. Henry J., AB, *Clerical Dress and Insignia of the Roman Catholic Church*, Milwaukee, WI: Bruce Publishing Co., 1945.

Messorio, Vittorio, *The Ratzinger Report*, San Francisco, CA: Ignatius Press, 1985.

New American Bible, New York, NY: Catholic Book Publishing Co., 1970.

Paul VI, Pope, *Sacrum Diaconatus Ordinem*, Washington, D.C.: United States Catholic Conference, 1967.

Permanent Deacons in the United States: Guidelines on Their Formation and Ministry, National Conference of Catholic Bishops, Washington, D.C.: United States Catholic Conference, 1985.

Schamoni, Wilhelm, *Married Men as Ordained Deacons*, London: Burns and Oates, 1955.

Shaw, Russell, *Permanent Deacons*, 1986 Revision, Washington, D.C.: United States Catholic Conference, 1986.